ETHICS

ETHICS

VOLUME 1

*Basic Elements and Methodology
in an Ethical Theology*

TRUTZ RENDTORFF

Translated by
Keith Crim

FORTRESS PRESS   PHILADELPHIA

Translated from the German *Ethik: Grundelemente, Methodologie und Konkretionen einer ethischen Theologie*, Band 1 (Stuttgart: W. Kohlhammer Verlag, 1980).

Library of Congress Cataloging-in-Publication Data

Rendtorff, Trutz.
    Ethics.

    Translation of: Ethik.
    Contents: v. 1. Basic elements and methodology in an ethical theology.
    1. Christian ethics. I. Title.
BJ1253.R4413 1986   241   85-45484
ISBN 0-8006-0767-8 (v. 1)

K899J85 Printed in the United States of America 1-767

Contents

Preface to the American Edition

The German version of this work was published in 1980 (vol. 1) and 1982 (vol. 2), almost at the same time as James Gustafson's *Ethics from a Theocentric Perspective* (vol. 1, 1981). Now that the American edition of my book is appearing, I would like to comment briefly on the relation between our respective concepts of theological ethics, as I see it.

James Gustafson explained the meaning of his work by "An Interpretation of Our Circumstances," in which he discussed aspects of culture, religion, the theological scene, and of Christian and philosophical ethics. In my book a comparable discussion can be found in Part I, "The Place of Ethics," and in Part III, "Methodology of Ethics." After reading Professor Gustafson's book, I feel tempted to enter into a discussion of his concept of ethics and to make the dialogue with North American theology and ethics explicit. This preface is not the place to yield to this temptation. Nevertheless a few, brief comments may be in order by way of presenting my work as it makes its way from a rather parochial language into the world's leading language.

The intention to conceive ethics as a basic dimension of theology seems to be a point of common interest. In my book, this intention is characterized by the term "ethical theology." In his book, Gustafson says that "the theological direction of this work bears similarities to the turn taken by many of the theologians earlier in the present century" (p. 84) and he names Karl Barth, Henry Nelson Wieman, and H. Richard Niebuhr. Under the circumstances of continental theology the long-lasting dominance of Karl Barth's dogmatic theology has placed theological ethics into the shadow of dogmatics. Thus, the likelihood of an autonomous theological ethics in open dialogue with other disciplines and with different world views was diminished. It is obvious that the "turn" to which Gustafson alludes had a different

meaning and led to other consequences under the respective circumstances, but this would have to be debated in a comparison of the
North American and the continental history of theological thought in
this century. In my book, in any event, the element of opposition out-
weighs any similarity to that type of theology that is determined by
Karl Barth; but that does not at the same time exclude a certain closeness to the work of H. Richard Niebuhr.

In another respect it could be of some interest to compare how
Gustafson relates his "theocentric ethics" to tradition. His book, he
says, "is a Reformed theology, of sorts" (p. 157). And as a matter of
fact, it strikes the familiar original note of Calvinist theological
thought when he states: "The chief end of man . . . may be to honor,
to serve and to glorify (celebrate) God" (p. 113). His own intention
becomes clear when he confronts the "anthropocentrism" of the ethical and religious orientation in the West with his altered and radical
"theocentric focus of attention" (p. 112). If that is "Reformed theology, of sorts," then one might say of my ethical theology that it is a
"Lutheran theology, of sorts." There may be Lutheran theologians
who would not agree. But this book seeks to describe the basic structure of *human* life. Is that "anthropocentrism"? It does not necessarily
signify what is traditionally called subjectivism, but on the contrary
it aims at the recognition of the objective structure of the world of
human life that claims us as being God's world. To explain this relation is the task of an ethical theology.

The ethical debate in the churches and in Christianity takes place
in a historic world that is shaped by enduring theological traditions.
Ethical debates always imply debates over different world views.
That is what makes them often so fascinatingly opaque. Theological
ethics here has a task of enlightenment and of mediation. Gustafson
speaks with emphasis of our historic world as not being the whole of
reality. This provides a strong motive for conceptualizing theocentric
ethics as altering the traditional historical concept of ethics. In this
connection Gustafson quotes Ernst Troeltsch several times. The
incomplete and complex work of Ernst Troeltsch could indeed serve
as a helpful bridge on which theologians and ethicists could meet,
moving beyond their various historical circumstances in new ways. At
the end of his huge volume on *Historicism and Its Problems*, Ernst
Troeltsch formulated the program "to overcome history through history." Ethics is the place where continuity and change, as elements

in the experience of reality, become concrete themes that, over and over, are addressed in terms of human responsibility.

I wish to thank Dr. Keith Crim for the excellent translation and to express my gratitude to Fortress Press for publishing it.

Munich, July 1985   TRUTZ RENDTORFF

Foreword

"The starting place of all ethics is when a human being regards himself or herself as a task to be undertaken" (Wolfgang Trillhaas). The study of ethics consists in the study of the basic elements which confront us in this task. There is no general agreement about the place of ethics in the study of theology. On the contrary, it is a subject of considerable dispute. The only thing that is agreed upon is that ethics constitutes an important dimension of all theology, especially systematic theology. There are various ideas of how this is to be understood and what the basis of ethics as a theological discipline is. The interest in ethics works against finding such answers. The ethicist generally steps back from the academic discussion, dealing instead with current themes of ethical discourse and arousing the expectation that specific answers will be obtained from concrete questions. But the answers arrived at in this manner depend to a great extent on one's prior understanding of ethics.

For this reason this present attempt to develop an ethical theology begins by determining the place of ethical questions and then develops a view of the basic elements that constitute the reality of an ethical life in which the awareness of the ethical consciousness develops. For the study of ethics must first of all have as its content the formation of an ethical consciousness in order to be able within that structure to evaluate current ethical questions correctly. Therefore the student of theology must learn to regard ethics as a basic element of theology and to recognize the autonomy of the ethical dimension of theology.

To be sure, the theologian does not enter the field of ethics alone, but becomes involved in competition and conversation with many others. A fruitful discussion with other academic disciplines demands a carefully formulated methodology, with the help of which we can carry out the debate concerning the ethical relevance of our interpretations of reality and then incorporate these interpretations into an ethical theology. This interdisciplinary dialogue must always be related to the basic issues that the ethical questions must confront, even in the consideration of methodology. This also involves identifying the issues in the dialogue and determining the order in which they are to be considered. Moreover, in the interests of providing guidance for the student, a clear overview must always be kept in mind.

The basic elements of the ethical reality of life and the methodology of ethics are the tools with which we can explicate concrete ethical issues. These issues then enable us to define in a variety of ways the task of ethics and establish its normative value. Like all academic study, ethics calls for the patience which serious thought demands and which must be the schoolmaster to the impatient desire to obtain results that have immediate application. In keeping with its goals, such an ethic concentrates on elementary arguments and analyses which can serve as model procedures.

I wish to express my thanks to the participants in my seminar at the University of Munich for their stimulating discussion of the first draft of this book. I am especially grateful to Dr. Friedrich W. Graf for his advice and assistance in the preparation of the final form of the book and to Herbert Will for his careful preparation of the manuscript and for his help in proofreading. I am also grateful to Mrs. Editha Sauer for her care and diligence in checking the printer's proofs. This first volume, which deals with the place of ethics, its basic elements, and its methodology will be followed by a second volume dealing with the concrete issues of ethics.

Munich, 24 January 1980   TRUTZ RENDTORFF

THE PLACE OF ETHICS

PART ONE

THE ... OF ETHICS

1. The Current Ethical Situation as a Task of Theology

a. What Is Ethics?

Ethics is the theory of the conduct of human life.

We speak of ethics in order to give expression to the experience that the world in which we live, with all its many relationships, demands that we take a stand. Ethical questions are life questions that people encounter in the process of living and to which they must respond in the reality of their own lives. All activity implies such a taking of positions. Human activity is never a merely external relationship to or a manipulation of objects. Human activities involve a relationship to the reality in which humans always find themselves, which determines who they are, and which places them under obligations. The awareness of the inner responsibility involved in the reality of human life finds expression in the questions of ethics.

In this sense ethics can be termed an intensified form of the human experience of reality, insofar as the theme of ethics is participation through one's own conduct in the reality that confronts us with its demands.

Ethics as the theory of the conduct of human life involves therefore the ethical meaning of the reality in which persons live and participate as active agents. It involves our dealings with the ethical question and the presuppositions and goals which govern the positions that persons take. It involves the question of what constitutes the good life, a question which is not answered by the conduct of daily life, but which arises wherever persons are required to make a commitment.

These introductory observations on the theme of ethics must be examined thoroughly and in detail. Then in that light we must look at the present ethical situation. For ethics as the theory of the conduct of human life is constantly called forth by concrete life situations that give rise to ethical questions. Ethics has no other body of data. Moreover ethical reflection is by no means the exclusive preserve of theoreticians. Human life continuously unfolds as a permanent ethical discussion, and in a certain sense everyone is involved in it. Ethical questions of greater or lesser significance are explored everywhere, because they are implicit in every situation of life and activity. Granted, this daily ethical discourse is generally in response to a specific issue. It is intertwined with the institutional life of families, schools, churches, and political and social institutions. It arises through the life experiences of young and old, through love and friendship, through strictly personal encounters and relationships and through broader, impersonal ones. It can be and is carried on in some manner in every area of human life. Public debates about the goals of our actions and the manner in which responsibility is borne or abused sets ethical discourse in motion. It needs a lively and often sharp debate in order to test the significance of issues and points of view and to bring newly discovered themes into the ongoing ethical discussion.

The theory of ethics is involved in this discussion, for otherwise its special and specific task would be meaningless. But it stands somewhat apart from the discussion that takes place in the daily conduct of life. This is in order that we may keep an eye on the structure of the ethical question and on the foundations and goals which play a role in the varied concrete situations of life, and that we may reflect on the nature of the positions that are taken and on the extent of the influence which they will have. There is especial need for a theory of ethics wherever there are tendencies to radicalize ethical questions, tendencies that involve the understanding of the reality implied in those questions.

b. The Present Ethical Situation

The distinctive characteristic of ethical discourse in the present day is that ethical questions are no longer limited to the relationship of individuals to the world in which they live, but have as their theme the structure of that world itself. The tendency to radicalize ethical questions in this manner manifests itself in various areas, some outstanding examples of which may be mentioned here. In reference to the form of human society which brings individuals together, we see that the ethically binding form of the state is no longer regarded without question as the primary basis for political relationships and activities. Instead politics itself becomes the theme in determining the basis of the state. This is seen with particular clarity in that political and social revolution has become a symbol for the attitude toward that reality of human life which governs relationships among individuals. This undermines the traditional starting point of the institutional form of a common political life under law and the forms of acknowledged authority. This has produced a crisis which demands that new positions be taken that go far beyond the obvious pros and cons of revolutionary slogans. We find we must take ethical positions not only in order to solve specific problems defined in terms of political responsibility in specific political relationships, but also in dealing with the question of the relevance of political life itself.

When we look at the shape of the personal life of the individual we see that sexual issues and questions of life style in reference to marriage and family have brought about changes in circles strongly influenced by tradition, changes that only a few decades ago would hardly have seemed possible. It is impossible to overestimate the extraordinarily dramatic manner in which these transformations have taken place in the realm of family life and in the relationship of the generations to each other. The institutions of marriage and family as the locus of the ethical form of sexual behavior have been subjected to critical standards and concepts that seek to make the recognition of those institutions independent of any autonomous claim to determine the orientation of sexual self-realization. In this area as well the symbol we see is that of a sexual *revolution*. The reconstruction of standards of binding and enduring relationships is a new task that confronts us. And the physical and social nature of the reality of the person in every relationship is the theme of that task.

In questions involving our relationship to the world around us, a new consciousness of environmental concerns has emerged. This is the result of the concentrated concern of sociological predictions and popular protest movements, which were significantly influenced by the activities and the studies of the "Club of Rome." This movement also involves the demand for a new and far-reaching reorientation of our understanding of reality. What seems at first to be only a concern for clean lakes and rivers, clear air, and streets free of noise is extrapolated as the dramatic question of the future of humanity on this planet. It should be clearly noted that activities undertaken in reference to questions arising out of the realities of human life have become radicalized in categories of a revolution in our world view and in our understanding of reality. But the loud "No!" of rejection and reorientation is only one of the preliminaries to the formulation of new positions in human affairs, and it must be transformed by the insight that even global crises can be defined and solved concretely only by purposeful activity that takes account of the realities.

What these examples have in common is that they testify to a historical and social transformation that takes the form of a demand for a new, transformed attitude and position. They involve both the conduct of human life and the understanding of the realities of that life in its totality. But the change in ethical norms and orientations by no means marks their end; on the contrary it calls for increased attentiveness to the basic structures of ethical responsibility even amid that change.

The pressure of contemporary problems and the demand for innovation also involve ethical theory and raise the question of the direction such theory should move. Thus the theoretical task is first of all to gain an overview of the status of ethical questions in the movements of our time and to identify amid the currents of the epoch the basic elements of the ethical reality of human life. But the theoretical task cannot remain neutral and disinterested. It always involves the practical task of determining what causes it should and must promote, what it must question critically, and what tendencies it must oppose. It is therefore not surprising that ethical theory finds itself today in a lively process of clarification. The arena in which the task of ethical theory is concerned above all becomes clear, however, only when a further example is added to those given above as topics for the ethical discourse of the present time.

Ethical discourse takes on a dramatic form when its differing motifs come together in the demand that humanity itself become something other than what it is, when on various sides propaganda for a "new" humanity is advanced, and at the same time there are demands for the elimination of the "old" humanity. Here too the revolutionary symbol has found expression in the formula of an "anthropological revolution." A demand of this nature and of this extent raises at once the question of who will be the object of such a revolution and who will lead it — in short, who is to be revolutionized by whom. The demand can indicate extreme danger when certain people and their programs lay claim to the right to transform others into the picture of the new humanity as the objects of the revolution. The meaning, if any, of such a demand can only be that all humanity must see itself involved in the experiences of the transformation. The ethical question becomes, in a radical manner, the question that humanity asks concerning its own nature. To this question there is no answer in the form of direct suggestions and instructions for action. Thus talk of an anthropological revolution can have only metaphorical meaning, and everything depends on the aspect in which it is at all possible to have a sound basis for speaking of such a revolution. Theology must take the position that humanity's question about itself must be the question concerning human reality in general and therefore the question, who then constitutes the reality of humanity? Theology must approach this question and develop it in such a way as to express the essential relationship of all human reality to God. In dealing with this basic ethical question of our time theology must lead the way by formulating the question in a manner that truly accords with reality.

c. The Task of an Ethical Theology

If humans are not to become the objects of the will of other humans who want to force them to change, then it is essential that the ethical question be regarded with all seriousness as a question concerning human life itself and not subsumed under specific finite, conditioned aspects of the way human life is conducted. Thus theology has the primary task of introducing into ethical discourse a frame of reference in which questions can be posed in a manner appropriate to the reality of human life. It must therefore insist that the theological dimension of that reality play a role in providing enlightenment and orientation. The experience of change and the resultant radicalization of the question which humanity asks about itself are indications that human life is not something that exists in and of itself, but rather depends in an elementary fashion on the social nature of life. It cannot be thoroughly understood through an exhaustive examination of the relationships of human beings to one another and to their environment, but has as its basis the relationship of all reality to God. It is in the challenge to act and to take a stand that the basic communicative structure of the world of human affairs is experienced. Therefore action is always a response to human life in society. The communicative structure of the reality of life is in its essence that of a life in communion with God. In ethics the recognition of this basic situation is at issue. The task of an ethical theology is to provide an explication and a basis for this state of affairs and to support it through argumentation.

Ethics is thus an intensified form of theology, because the relevant

and contemporary ethical questions force us to confront in an intensified manner the question of the basis and goal of the reality of human
life.

Defining the place of ethics today demands therefore that theology
raise and define anew the ethical question in its basic structure,
which is just as much present in the many questions and problems of
daily discourse as it is in the further questions of the structure of our
world view. There was a time when it could be maintained that dogmatic theology was difficult and complicated. It could become clear,
simple, and comprehensible only when one's attention turned to
ethics and all the dogmatic ballast was left behind. Such a concept
appears naive today. The characteristics of the present ethical age of
Christianity include not only constantly increasing differentiation of
the questions that claim public attention, but also a significant
change of themes. It is one of the characteristics of the contemporary
ethical scene that the ethical question is an intensified form of the
search for reality. If ethics is accepted as the theme and task of theology, then theology's self-investigation is set in motion anew. It must
examine itself to see how far and in what manner it can fulfill its
claim to be a discipline that deals with reality.

But in what sense is this valid? One point of view says that theology
must concern itself more with the realities of life and expand its
themes and concepts by drawing on the knowledge and insights
which have been gained in other academic disciplines. Therefore
there is a wide-spread demand that for the sake of ethics, theology
must enter into an interdisciplinary dialogue with other academic
fields. This is necessary if we are to be able to grasp concretely, in all
their dimensions, the reality of the experiences of life, in the context
of which ethical questions arise. But the cultivation of interdisciplinary contacts will remain something merely external as long as it is not
clear what distinctive basis theology has for dealing with reality.
Otherwise a mere supplementing of ethics with all sorts of information would remain a purely superficial exercise. The methodological
questions which arise here deserve closer attention. But they must be
approached from a concept of ethical reality that is anchored in a
theological understanding of its own discipline. This touches on basic
issues in the position of theology in the context of modern life.

In historical perspective the radicalization of the ethical question as the
question which humanity asks concerning itself has come to be posed in such

a manner that it can be answered only in terms of humanity and human actions. Thus it would seem that one of the features of the ethical question is a strict distinction between it and all theology.

At least as early as the second half of the nineteenth century ethics was programmatically formulated in terms of an emancipation in principle from all theology and religion. The theology of the twentieth century has responded to this attempt at emancipation with the thesis that when theology is correctly understood it must be sharply distinguished from all human ethics. If ethics is to be practiced at all it must be only as a dogmatic discipline. An independent ethics could only be, theologically, erroneous.

A historical example of a program for an ethics emancipated from religion and theology can be seen in the work of Friedrich Jodl, who presented his history of ethics as a modern philosophical discipline, but involving in specific sections a relationship of ethics and religion. He portrays how the independence of ethics from religion and theology constantly increased in the history of modern ethics. (Friedrich Jodl, *Geschichte der Ethik als philosophische Wissenschaft*, 2 vols., reprinted 1965). Jodl was a committed participant in the struggle for the emancipation of ethics from religion. Moreover, as a propagandist for this emancipation and as one of the founders in 1892 of the German Society for Ethical Culture, he worked hard to achieve it. See H. Lübbe, *Säkularisierung. Geschichte eines ideenpolitischen Begriffes*, 1965, pp. 41–44.

But the antithesis of modern ethics and theology was also a basic concept of dialectic theology in the first half of this century. This served to strengthen and support certain features of the religious thought-world in theological discussions. For a discussion of the connections involved, see Christof Gestrich, *Neuzeitliches Denken und die Spaltung der dialektischen Theologie*, 1977.

Under the dominance of the understanding of these two realms as alternatives, the debate about the basic ethical issues within theology was to a large extent carried on as a debate about the independence of theology and the boundary between it and the rest of the intellectual world. In this manner the question of the significance of ethics as a proper dimension of theology was pushed into the background in the interest of an autonomous understanding of theology.

In German Protestant theology there are two exceptions that are concerned with the freedom of access of an independent theology to ethical problems: W. Trillhaas, *Ethik*, 3d ed., 1971; and Knud E. Løgstrup, *Die ethische Forderung*, 1959.

Ethics is an intensified form of theology, because it expands the themes of the question which is basic to all theology, that of the structure of our relations to reality. Thus ethics does not abolish theology, but makes it necessary in a manner that is new and fresh.

One indication of this is that the concepts "theology" and "ethics," as far as their subject matter is concerned, can be used synonymously today. Thus it is no accident that expressions such as political "theology," "theology" of sexuality, ecological "theology" are used, even though it would be just as appropriate to speak of political ethics, sexual ethics, or environmental ethics. The need to speak in this context of "theology" can be regarded as an expression of the concern to show that it is not just a matter of special ethical questions, but of questions and problems that touch on our whole understanding of reality and thus have as their content more than questions of normative behavior and correct actions.

J. B. Metz has recently reintroduced the concept of a political theology into the discussion (J. B. Metz, *Zur Theologie der Welt*, 1968, and the continuation of the discussion in *Glaube in Geschichte und Gesellschaft*, 1977). On the controversy over the relationship of political theology and political ethics, see H. Peukert, ed., *Zur Diskussion der politschen Theologie*, 1969. On the wider discussion see A. Seifart, *Der Gott der politschen Theologie*, 1978. H. Ringeling's *Theologie und Sexualität*, 1966, is an important and basic ethical discussion of sexuality. The term "ecological theology" is presented by G. Liedtke, *Im Bauch des Fisches. Eine ökologische Theologie*, 1979.

In any case, the present stage of the discussion can no longer be appropriately comprehended by seeing ethics and theology as alternatives. We must abandon the tendency this implies of either absorbing or subordinating ethics in such a way that it suggests that theology has an exclusive claim to ethics. The task of the theologians is to bring their discipline to bear on the fundamental questions posed by ethics. This task leads to the construction of an ethical theology that develops the framework for ethics as the theory of how human life is to be lived. The Protestant ethical tradition is free from scholasticism and has no fixed pedagogical structure. It has a much more limited body of fixed theoretical positions than is the case in dogmatics, with its old Protestant canon of fixed themes and distinctions that constitute a body of knowledge on which the student of theology is to be examined, and which present the challenge of applying them to the present day. The theoretical task of an ethical theology is to give prominence to the basic structure of the ethical question, to identify its theological elements, to bring together in a methodologically defined manner the various aspects which play a role in the concretization of the themes of ethics, and thus to prepare the way for understanding of the concrete issues of ethics.

A good example of this open situation for the investigation of ethics within theology can be found in a comparison of the two textbooks in ethics presently used in Sweden: G. Wingren, ed., *Etik och kristen Tro*, 1971; R. Holte, et. al. *Etiska Problem*, 1970. While Wingren's book is constructed on historical lines that allow the various theological disciplines to have their way, Holte's book follows a different model of ethical argument by adopting the Anglo-Saxon tradition of analytical ethics.

2. Ethics as an Intellectual Discipline

a. The Place of Ethics Within Theology

"The basic ethical questions are also basic questions of theology." We must now inquire into the meaning of this statement and into the role of the expression "ethical theology" which has been employed here. This involves the place of ethics within the whole theoretical structure of theology as an academic discipline. In terms of the history of theology it involves taking a position in the quarrel over the relationship between ethics and dogmatics. In terms of the theory of knowledge, it involves the sources of ethical insight in theology.

The statement that the basic ethical questions are also the basic questions of theology is meant in the following sense: In the modern period the discipline of theology has become differentiated into a multiplicity of areas of research, and it has built up in its teaching an extensive and specialized canon. The statement has the same validity for all the principal areas of research and specialities of theology, namely, that all the basic questions are also the basic questions of theology. The basic questions of historical exegesis are, in their methodology and content, basic questions of theology, for example, in terms of a theological hermeneutic. The basic questions of historical theology and of the history of the church and of Christianity are basic questions of theology, for example, in terms of a theological discipline of history. The same can be said in similar manner of dogmatic theology, or of practical theology, or of general religious studies and the philosophy of religion. If this state of affairs is recognized it is then possible to perceive the basic questions of theology in each of the various fields of research and in the various principle areas of specialization. The unity of theology as a discipline will not be represented by a single specific area to which all other areas and fields of research will be subordinated. Rather the unity of theology will be perceived thematically in the presuppositions that constitute the material of the various areas and fields of research, and thematically in the goals of theological work toward which the research and the teaching of the various disciplines are oriented.

The relationships of the various areas of research in theology to each other as described here corresponds to the actual state of theology and thus can be assumed without further justification. To be sure, the question can be raised whether there is an adequate and satisfying basis for this state of theology. It is always appropriate to raise such doubts, because any discipline that is differentiated in so pronounced a manner is always under obligation to raise the question of its own unity. But wherever this is explicitly done the result is not that the differentiated nature of theology disappears, but that it is interpreted. The reason for this is that it clearly corresponds to the differentiation of the whole realm of Christian life in history and the present.

The most recent attempts to interpret the encyclopedic nature of theology are G. Ebeling, *Studium der Theologie. Eine enzyklopädische Orientierung* (UTB, 446); W. Pannenberg, *Wissenschaftstheorie und Theologie*, 1973 [*Theology and the Philosophy of Science*, 1976].

1) *The Relationship of Ethics to Dogmatics*

On the basis of the presuppositions outlined above, we must inquire into the special relationship of ethics to dogmatics. For both are areas of research and bodies of doctrine within systematic theology. In terms of history and content their relationship has been determined through manifold thematic connections and areas of overlap, but also through the problem of drawing distinctions between them and delimiting the area of each. It is especially true for ethics and dogmatics, as it is true in the overview of all theology, that all areas of research and specialization have by their very nature many and varied relationships to each other.

This history of the relationship between ethics and dogmatics, their distinctive connections and limits, as well as the problems of content that unite them has recently been presented in an expert manner by H. J. Birkner. See H. J. Birkner, "Das Verhältnis von Dogmatik und Ethik" in *Handbuch der christlichen Ethik*, vol. 1, 1978, pp. 281–96. See also N. H. G. Robinson, *The Groundwork of Christian Ethics*, 1975.

By accepting the proposition that the basic questions of ethics are at the same time those of theology, we do not mean that ethics should be subordinated to dogmatics, but rather that ethics in its own way, quite distinct from that of dogmatics, comprehends the basic problems of theology, and therefore with dogmatics jointly represents the realm of systematic theology. The use of the term "ethical theology" is intended to express this relationship of ethics to its task. It also implies a specific decision which must be justified and developed in detail in the construction of an ethic. Specifically, this distinction means that in dealing with its basic questions ethics is not bound by the explication of the specific themes and historic controversies of dogmatics, but must independently deal with the basic questions of theology in a manner that is related to the ethical realities of life. This accords with the way in which systematic theology is understood today. Its proper task is not seen as exclusively that of developing dogmatic theology, and therefore it increasingly frames its basic questions — in dependence on the terminology of Catholic theology — in terms of the task of a "fundamental theology." This indicates a wider and less limited horizon for the discussion of basic theological questions, in contrast to the narrow delimitations of areas of specialization.

Several works can be cited for an understanding within Protestant theology of systematic theology as fundamental theology: G. Ebeling, "Erwägungen zu einer evangelischen Fundamentaltheologie" in ZThK 67 (1970): 479–524; W. Joest, *Fundamentaltheologie*, 1974; W. Pannenberg, *Wissenschaftstheorie und Theologie*, 1973, pp. 299ff. [*Theology and the Philosophy of Science*, 1976]. This development corresponds to the use of the term "fundamental theology" in Catholic moral theology in order to gain independent access to the basic questions of theology. See especially F. Böckle, *Fundamentalmoral*, 1977 [*Fundamental Moral Theology*, 1980].

The motifs which led to a more open understanding of systematic theology can be seen in a statement of Schleiermacher, in which he took a clear position on the relationship of ethics and dogmatics. "Although morality has been emancipated from dogmatics, the impression remains that it is subordinated to it. This impression is especially harmful because it involves moral discourse in whatever quarrels the dogmatics of a given time concerns itself with. It is not as if there were not any differences, but they are of another sort, so that in our churches we may have the same moral teaching, even under differing dogmatic systems. Thus there must be something original to which both disciplines can be traced back. Clearly there was a Christian life before there was a Christian moral teaching. But where did this Christian life come from? Out of the Christian faith, to be sure, but from none other than that which is also prior to Christian doctrine. . . . Thus we should not

trace the statements of our moral beliefs back to dogmatic statements, but
to that on which these are based." F. Schleiermacher, *Die christliche Sitte
nach den Grundsätzen der evangelischen Kirche im Zusammenhange dar-
gestellt*, ed. L. Jonas, *Werke* I, 12, 2d ed. 1884, p. 24 (1st ed. 1826/7).

Liberation of ethics from dogmatics does not mean liberation from
theology. We have already spoken of how and why ethics is to be
understood as an intensified form of theology, and have introduced
the term "ethical theology" in this connection. The discussions of the
relationship of ethics and dogmatics reveal the suspicion that an ethic
independent of dogmatics is a sign of an attempt to liberate humans
from the authority of the divine revelation and the teachings of the
church. The criticism involved here is just as applicable to the independence of exegetical, historical, and practical theology. It grows
out of the concept that dogmatics covers the whole of theology. But
in the light of the actual structure of theology this concept is not relevant substantively nor methodologically. It is in reality the expression
of a specific problem and should therefore be expressly dealt with
here.

In a manner that has had far-reaching consequences for modern
Protestant theology, Karl Barth insisted that theology is identical
with "church dogmatics," and that for that reason ethics also should
be taught only under the protection of dogmatics. The arguments he
presented are highly relevant to the question under consideration
here, that of the extent to which the basic questions of ethics are also
those of theology. (See K. Barth, *Church Dogmatics*, vol. I, 1, 1935
(E. T. 19) and also II, 2, 1942 (E. T. 19). The following quotations
are taken from Vol. II, 2.)

In his *Dogmatics*, Barth accorded to "general ethics" a place following and continuing the doctrine of God. The doctrine of God "is
to be explicitly depicted, developed, and explained as ethics" (p. 572).
The prerogative of dogmatics is shown in that Barth begins with the
"Answering of the ethical problem" (p. 575). For him the answer lies
in that human "self-determination" is subordinate to God's
"predetermination." Thus Barth includes under ethics the "question
of human life" which is posed by human existence. This is entirely in
agreement with the approach that we have selected here for ethics.
But Barth so combines the "question of life" with the superiority of
"dogmatics" over "ethics" that this question can have no status as a
proper question, but can be legitimate only on the basis of its theolog-

ical answer. And in the case where the question itself is taken as the starting point, Barth sees the ethicist as traveling a theological bypath. Thus Barth can say that the human "attempts to answer it (this question)" (p. 583) must ultimately be regarded as "sin." "Sin" is the human attempt "to provide from one's own resources" the answer to the question of what constitutes good and evil. And the attempts to provide a human answer to this question mean that man "sinned in becoming an ethicist" (p. 573).

Barth's argument here results in his taking "God" and "man" as analogous to the working concepts "dogmatics" and "ethics." As a result, "dogmatics" and "ethics" constitute so great a contrast that "God" and "man" seem to be in direct competition with each other. But according to Barth's own theology that is not possible at all, but indeed quite impossible.

For this reason, when we consider the determination of the proper place of ethics and dogmatics in reference to scholarly theory and methodology, such a line of reasoning leads to major misunderstandings. Basically it can be understood only when interpreted in terms of the debate which Barth conducted with other theological positions. When we once leave aside the polemical relationship to contemporary issues, then Barth, with his subordination of ethics under dogmatics, has raised the genuine problem of the manner in which the basic questions of ethics are also the basic problems of theology. He approached this problem from the side of dogmatics and therefore expressed the position that dogmatics always has also an ethical significance. For dogmatics presents in its own way the explication of those reasons or factors which compel humans to take a position on this question that is posed by life itself. If we ask why dogmatics has an interest in ethics, we encounter a problem inherent in ethics, namely, ethics cannot simply be regarded as identical with a theory of human actions. Already at the start of this discussion we pointed out the reasons for this. Later they will be considered in detail (Part Two: The Three Basic Elements of the Ethical Reality of Life). But then the subordination of ethics to dogmatics, as demanded by Barth, must be seen in another light. It means that ethics is not merely a teaching about actions. It contains presuppositions about reality, which must also be explicitly discussed. But this insight by no means leads necessarily to a demand that ethics be subordinated to dogmatics. For the final result of doing so would be that the knowledge and the carrying out of the dogmatic arguments as they have developed in the history of Christian theology would be made the condition for ethics. But should such a dogmatism become the condition for doing ethics, then the same demand would extend to a transformation of dogmatics, such as that which has taken place in the openness to systematic theology as fundamental theology.

Barth himself says repeatedly that dogmatics has an ethical significance. In the progressive development of his *Dogmatics* he modified this more profoundly in the direction of an ethical theology, than has so far been generally recognized. In his book *The Ethics of Karl Barth*, 1971, Robert E. Willis points to "a certain fluidity of the terms 'dogmatics' and 'ethics' in that they are to some extent interchangeable" (p. 193). But this "interchangeability" can also lead to specific misunderstandings, when an undisputed dogmatic authority is claimed for ethical judgments, as can often be observed in Barth's work, and above all, as it has become a theological gesture of many of his disciples. Anyone who lays claim to the ethical significance of dogmatics must also make this explicit on the plain of ethical reflection and assume responsibility for doing so. On Barth in reference to this point see T. Rendtorff, "Der ethische Sinn der Dogmatik" in *Realisierung der Freiheit. Beiträge zur Kritik der Theologie K. Barths*, 1976, ed. T. Rendtorff.

When we look back on the debate launched by Barth, we must say that its theological motifs can be apprehended more accurately and relevantly when they are separated from the question of a relationship of subordination between dogmatics and ethics. In contrast to the special form of dogmatic theology, ethical theology must plead for an openness of theological thought to that reality of life in which ethical questions arise. Barth's position, at least in its most sharply formulated statements, has the result that theological ethics in its dogmatic form permits no further debate. Rather, in the place of discussion, it confronts "other" concepts of ethics with the "final word," "beyond which discussion may not proceed" (p. 575). Indeed, it is the specific weakness of an ethic which is subordinated to dogmatics that it is forced to think and speak in an apodictic and authoritarian manner, and thus is no longer able to assume the obligation of being capable of entering into dialogue, precisely in the field of ethics. It is highly significant that it is not possible to conceive of an ethic in which the question of whether or not the elementary responsibilities of the realities of human life are really relevant remains an open question. An ethical theology must then deal in its own way with the fact that the givenness of life, which is the presupposition for human actions, constitutes the elementary context of reality in which the questions of how human life should be conducted arise. The theological task of ethics is the reconstruction of the question which life itself poses for us and which we are obliged to answer. The ethicist must understand this question in a manner that makes it clear that the question which humans ask about themselves involves humanity in its relation to God. "In relation to God" means, first and foremost, that it involves humanity under all circumstances and, that beyond the limits of all specific areas of action, involves human life in its totality. But this cannot mean that the question concerns humanity in a manner that is isolated from the experiences of life and that runs counter to those experiences. For it is precisely the experience of the reality of life that makes us aware of the ethical question as such and demands that human beings take a stand in the midst of the concrete realities of life.

If ethics has an independent position within systematic theology that contrasts to dogmatics, then the question arises anew of the relationship of ethics to the normative historical sources of Christian theology, and first of all to the writings of the New Testament.

2) *The Relationship of Ethics to New Testament Exegesis*

Exegetical research has again and again exalted the ethics found in the writings of the New Testament. Therefore it cannot be the task of ethical theology to enter into competition with exegetical research. But in reference to the approach and the goals of theological ethics the concern must be to seek to make sure that at least in the basics it is in agreement with the results of exegetical research. Here through examples and within appropriately brief compass our position must be defined. In the individual steps through which a basis for ethics is established these issues will be discussed in more detail.

The explanations of New Testament ethics in contemporary exegetical literature yield a relatively unified picture. It cannot and should not be our purpose here to enter into the details of the ethical discussion, but we can look at some examples of the basic features of the consensus of exegetes as to method and content. The relevant literature includes H. D. Wendland, *Ethik des Neues Testamentes* (NTD, supplementary vol. 4), 1970; W. Schrage, *Die konkreten Einzelgebote in der paulinisches Paränese*, 1961; and "Barmen II und das Neue Testament" in *Zum politischen Auftrag der christlichen Gemeinde. Barmen II*, 1974, pp. 127–71; O. Merk, *Handeln aus*

Glauben. Die Motivierungen der paulinischen Ethik, 1968; G. Strecker, *Handlungsorientierter Glaube. Vorstudien zu einer Ethik des Neuen Testaments,* 1972. The following discussion is based on the summarizing studies of R. Becker in "Das Problem der Schriftgemässheit der Ethik," in *Handbuch der christlichen Ethik,* vol. 1, pp. 243–68 and G. Strecker, "Strukturen einer neutestamentlichen Ethik" in *ZThK* 75 (1978): 117–36.

The answer of historical-exegetical research to the question of whether there is a unified New Testament ethic may be summarized as follows. The Synoptic Gospels present a picture different from that found in the New Testament Epistles. The form itself of the texts transmitted in the canon forbids us to seek for a thoroughly rational and systematic program of ethical instruction as the purpose of these witnesses. The concrete language related to the specific situations, as well as the variety of forms and content of the New Testament writings, leads to the conclusion that the ethical interests of the first Christian generation had the goal of providing "helps for orienting conduct that is determined by faith and the Spirit and is related to specific situations in a critical manner. It has its foundations in the sense of responsibility of individuals and congregations and not in prescribed law" (Becker, 244). This consciously relativizing interpretation can free us to see the specific elements that give Christian ethics its distinctive structure. G. Strecker says much the same thing: "The New Testament as a whole can be understood as the document that records the attempt of the Christian faith to orient itself" (p. 145). Thus at the outset there is an explanation of why it is not possible to derive a sharply defined, catechism-like ethic from the New Testament, an ethic that as such would enable us to define a dogmatically accurate boundary between it and contemporary Jewish ethics or Hellenistic popular philosophy. Instead, historical study reveals that "The New Testament exhortation has its roots deep in the norms and values of its own time."

This context is also made explicit. Phil 4:8 can be regarded as the rule for Christian ethics, "Finally, brethren, whatever is true, whatever is honorable, whatever is just, whatever is pure, whatever is lovely, whatever is gracious, if there is any excellence, if there is anything worthy of praise, think about these things." The same rule is expressed in different words in Rom. 12:2, "Do not be conformed to this world, but be transformed by the renewal of your mind, that you may prove what is the will of God, what is good and acceptable and perfect." It is to this type of reflection and not to a fixed ethical canon

that Paul appeals, even in controversies within the church in reference to the struggles of the various Christian groups to assert themselves, "But test everything; hold fast what is good, abstain from
every form of evil" (1 Thess. 5:21–22).

This material leads to the conclusion that all New Testament documents have ethical significance. Early Christianity "placed the whole
conduct of life under a total, unified principle — Christian freedom"
(Becker, 245). In different phraseology the sum of the matter can be
expressed thus: "The distinctive feature of Christian ethics in the New
Testament is not an ethical program, but its Christological dimension. This is to be understood as a critical principle, for it brings into
question the tendency to legalism that inheres in every ethical system
and it provides the basis for the freedom to make ethical decisions"
(Strecker, 137). The contextual nature of the freedom of the Christian
faith marks a difference from the strict reliance on a legal code that
was characteristic of the ethical nature of Judaism. It is precisely the
radical formulation of individual legal stipulations, as was distinctive
for the proclamation of Jesus, that presents the spirit of the law as the
expression of God's will in contrast to the letter of the law. This is seen
in the antitheses of the Sermon on the Mount, in Jesus' relation to the
sabbath and to marriage, and in his position on material possessions.
Everywhere the "basic meaning" is "freedom based on trust in God's
care for us as our creator" (Becker, 252). The place where this freedom is authenticated is in the conduct of the Christian life. Therefore
the primary concern is not differentiation from others but the fact
that we belong to God, and this has primarily inclusive implications.
This holds both for the relationship to the Jewish tradition and for
that with the surrounding world of pagan religion. Selective borrow-
ing, a reflective eclecticism, is the hallmark of the freedom found in
New Testament ethics. Even conversion to Christ is not a self-
authenticating demarcation marker; it does not lead to an exclusivistic mode of life. In any case, that is never the dominant tendency. It
is rather that conversion brings the Christian into the living context
of the world which God has created. Even the command to love,
which rightly can be singled out as a distinctive feature of Christian
ethics, is not to be considered the exclusive possession of the early
church. (Strecker, 143; Becker, ibid.) In sum, it is the consensus of the
exegetes "that New Testament ethics does not have a clearly unified
content." The orientation of New Testament ethics can be summed up
in statements such as: Christian freedom consists in "being present for

others, especially for the weak, not in living for oneself, but through Christ making use of one's talents in service for others." "In this Christianity was free from the compulsion to distinguish itself through the originality of its specific requirements, but instead it was focused on that which is common to all humanity" (Becker, 246).

There is one feature of New Testament theology, however, that must be stressed. It is of fundamental significance for our understanding of ethics, although it is basically only the outgrowth of a syntactical observation. It was first formulated and interpreted by R. Bultmann, and since then it has attained almost canonical authority for the interpretation of New Testament ethics. This observation is based on Gal. 5:25, for example, but can also be supported by numerous other texts, "If we live by the Spirit, let us also walk by the Spirit." Here we encounter an indicative and an imperative, and the indicative is the presupposition and basis for the imperative, as well as coming into its fulfillment through the imperative.

On the exegetical discussion see above all R. Bultmann, "Das Problem der Ethik bei Paulus" (1924), reprinted in *Das Paulusbild in der neueren deutschen Forschung*, 1964, 179–99; and also W. Schrage, *Barmen II*, op cit., pp. 128–43, and O. Merk, op. cit., pp. 4–42.

The relationship of indicative and imperative can be regarded as providing the formal structure of New Testament ethics. And the fact that this relationship is based in Christology has rightly led again and again to the use of this structure as the key to the ethical exegesis of the Christian doctrine of freedom.

Bultmann himself incorporated the structure of indicative and imperative into his existential interpretation of the New Testament when he wrote that "a human being can be and can become only that which he or she already is," and that "humans can lead their own lives only on the basis of the fact that they already participate in that which already belongs to them" ("Neues Testament und Mythologie" (1942) reprinted in *Kerygma und Mythos* I, 1948, p. 38). The terms "indicative" and "imperative" have found wide resonance in the ethical literature. For example, P. Althaus used the formula in his own way: "Indicative and imperative are inseparably bound together, and only when together do they witness to the reality of God's dealings with humanity" (*Grundriss der Ethik*, 2d ed., 1953, p. 11); E. Brunner wrote, "The indicative of the divine promise becomes the imperative of the divine command" (*Das Gebot und die Ordnungen*, 1939, p. 67 [The Divine Imperative, 1947]). The use of this terminology in discussion is also found in, for example, H. Thielicke, *Theologische Ethik* I, 3d ed., 1965, pp. 315–63; P. Tillich, "Das religiöse Fundament des moralischen Handelns," in *Gesammelte Werke* III, 1961, pp. 17, 19, etc.; P. Lehmann, *Ethik als Antwort*, 1966, pp. 152ff.

Since I will also follow this structure in the development of my ethics and in the presentation of the basic elements of the reality of the ethical life, this is not the place to explore its content in detail. But by way of conclusion it can be regarded as established that in this respect there is here a specific line of thought that is oriented to the New Testament and which must be followed in the structure of an ethical theology.

b. Ethical Theology and General Ethics

When theologians turn their attention to ethics they do not enter an uninhabited house in which they can settle down without regard to others who dwell there. They share this house with many other disciplines, especially with philosophy. In a manner analogous to the dispute over the relationship between dogmatics and ethics within theology there is also a history of controversy about the relationship between theological ethics and philosophical ethics. But in addition jurisprudence, the social sciences, history, psychology, and economics can and do claim a share in the themes dealt with in ethics. If the basic question which ethics deals with is posed for us by the reality of human life, then every discipline which is concerned with that reality will concern itself more or less explicitly with ethical themes. Therefore part of the task of an ethical theology will be not only to remain open in general to the various claims to competence in dealing with ethical issues, but also to define in method and content a distinctive place for the debate with nontheological discussions of ethics.

In Greek philosophy ethics explicitly became a distinct discipline in Aristotle through borrowings from and debate with Plato. The commentary of Thomas Aquinas on the *Nicomachean Ethics* of Aristotle was of decisive importance for the adoption of Aristotelian ethical theories in medieval theology. Part II of the *Summa Theologica*, building on this acceptance of Aristotle, was long the decisive factor in theological ethics, and still is today in the Catholic tradition of moral theology and its renewal.

Through Melanchthon's commentaries, Protestant theology was also involved in the adoption of Aristotelian ethics carried out in the history of philosophical ethics. Later it was influenced permanently by the philosophy of Kant and the debates with that philosophy. There are clear indications that the history of Christian ethics is inconceivable apart from the history of philosophical ethics.

This is not the appropriate place to explore the history of ethics and the relationship of theology and philosophy throughout that history. These brief comments serve only to draw attention to the fact that the distinctive and proper interest which theology has in ethics, and which it must have, cannot be an exclusivistic interest. Certainly from a historical perspective there is no reason and no basis for theology to lay exclusive claim to the field of ethics.

The literature on the history of ethics flourished in the age of history, that is, the nineteenth century. I will mention here only a few works of continuing importance. From the early decades of the century: C. F. Stäudlin, *Geschichte der philosophischen, ebräischen und christlichen Moral im Grundriss*, 1806; W. M. L. de Wette, *Allgemeine Geschichte der christlichen Sittenlehre*, 2 vols., 1819–21. In the last third of the century a large number of comprehensive works were written: W. Gass, *Geschichte der christlichen Ethik*, 3 vols., 1881–87; Chr. E. Luthardt, *Die antike Ethik und ihre geschichtliche Entwicklung*, 1887, and *Geschichte der christlichen Ethik*, 2 vols., 1888–93. The last major work is O. Dittrich, *Die Systeme der Moral. Geschichte der Ethik vom Altertum bis zur Gegenwart*, 4 vols., 1923–32, reprinted 1964.

Profound changes in the understanding of the history of Christian ethics in its philosophical and historical context can be seen in E. Troeltsch, *Die Soziallehren der christlichen Kirchen und Gruppen. Gesammelte Schriften*, vol. 1, 1911, reprinted 1965; see esp. pp. 965ff. [*Social Teaching of the Christian Churches*, 1931]. It is surely not by chance that no new attempts were made to write a comprehensive history of ethics after H. van Oyen, *Ethik des Alten Testaments. Geschichte der Ethik*, vol. 2, 1967. For since Troeltsch the questions that are relevant to the basis and development of ethics have undergone such thorough reformulation that the question of the history of ethics has been pushed to one side by the question of its systematic possibility and necessity. As early as the end of the nineteenth century G. Simmel contended that it was questionable "whether ethics could remain a distinct discipline at all." Some day it may no longer appear relevant to try to unite parts of highly different disciplines under this point of view. In reference to the development of the discipline he voiced the hope that "the time is not long distant when not even a single book will bear the simple title 'ethics,' in the way in which a book can simply be titled 'physics' " (*Einleitung in die Moralwissenschaft*, 1892–93, reprint of the fourth edition in 1964, p. iv). Like philosophical ethics in most recent years in the German speaking world, an independent interest in ethics is for theology not primarily an interest in its history but in the systematic investigation of its bases and the possibilities of its independent development. As representative at present of the revival of philosophical ethics we may mention the writing collected and edited by M. Riedel in *Rehabilitierung der praktischen Philosophie*, 2 vols., 1972–74.

The most important factor in the crisis in ethics and the reformulation of the task of ethics is undoubtedly the development of the modern social sciences and their influence on our understanding of the world of human society. The empirical approach of sociology has also given new vitality to the descriptive study of morality and moral teaching that has been widely practiced ever since the French Enlightenment. In his introduction to the German translation of David Riesman's then much discussed book, *The Lonely Crowd*, 1950 (German trans., 1958), H. Schelsky felt himself called upon to explore the question of whether sociology could claim to be an ethic. His conclusion was that an empirical sociology constitutes a sort of "indirect moral teaching" (p. 19). The openness of the present state of the discussion would indicate that it is not opportune to try to develop a definitive delimitation of the relationship of ethical theology to the non-theological discussions of ethics and the themes found there. The path that will be followed here is to incorporate various aspects of this discussion into the development of my ethics, as I shall attempt to do in Part III, "The Methodology of Ethics."

This procedure is guided by a specific theological motif which may be formulated as follows. If we start from the fact that the human world in all its dimensions demands that stands be taken, and that in so doing the theologically relevant dimensions of ethics must be considered, this inevitably has consequences for theological methodology. Theology must resist the temptation to address the theoretical and practical atheism of the world in such a manner as to suggest that only where the theological form of ethics is consciously present do we encounter theologically relevant issues involving the ethical reality of life. On the contrary theology must, as a consequence of its own premises, enter into an open debate with other theoretical approaches to the study of the reality of human life. Bonhoeffer was certainly right when he voiced his impression that we find ourselves in an unprecedented confrontation with the complex realities of concrete ethical questions (*Ethik*, I, 1949, p. 11). This holds also for the complexity of theoretical claims that are made on ethics. In its own limited way theology can contribute to the clarification of the extraordinarily complex and, in part, heterogenous aspects of the current situation in which the social sciences and other disciplines approach the question of ethics.

c. The Ethos of Ethics as an Academic Discipline

The study of ethics is the study of the reality of human life under the guiding point of view of the conduct of life. Ethics must be careful not to confuse the theory of how to conduct one's life with the concrete conduct of life itself. There is a dogmatism not only of theology but also of ethical theory. Therefore in laying a basis for ethics we must remain aware that there is also an ethos of ethics. This consists in the fact that ethical theory must always be aware that its function is to be a servant in relation to the concrete carrying out of one's life. The practical usefulness of ethical theory is that in relation to the current questions of how to conduct one's life it promotes freedom of conduct, of weighing alternatives, and of testing them so that individuals can make those decisions that are demanded of them in the conduct of their lives and can do so in the freedom of their humanity. The ethos of ethics contributes to our being able always to distinguish between individuals themselves and their conduct.

In this respect ethical theory can make its contribution to human dignity, so that men and women will be able to move in the realm between life and action, and to respond in freedom to the question that life poses for them. Freedom is in its essence protection from immediacy, that is, from being delivered up defenseless to the world of activities and affairs. Unless human beings are able to make use of such freedom, they cannot consider themselves as ethical agents. The ethos of ethics consists therefore in being able to give a practical and relevant form to the indicative of freedom in the face of the pressure of duty in situations that demand immediate action.

Ethics as a theoretical concern is thus the practical and relevant perception of the conduct of human life that contributes to our being able to move beyond the alternatives in which the debates about the right way to live are often solidified under the pressures of daily life. For this reason ethics as the express concern about the presuppositions and bases of life, as well as about life's goal and orientation, is itself obliged to take a stand. Specifically, it must take a stand in such a way that ethical questions remain possible and meaningful. In short, an ethic must be on the side of ethical reflection and dare not lose itself in commands and prohibitions that demand immediate action.

This is an ethic that has a scientific quality by which it deserves to be called "critical." Any ethic which itself fell into unmediated moralizing and in a programmatic manner invented simulated situations for decision making would thereby betray its specifically academic and scientific task and no longer have an appropriate perception of its own function.

Any contribution to scientific ethics must therefore also make clear in what sense it has a right to claim to be "critical." Criticism as a synonym for "scholarly research" has a tradition by virture of being criticism of authority. This motif was present from the birth of ethics in Greek philosophy. In their debates with the Sophists, Socrates and Plato took up the problem that the legitimation of morality through its origins, through custom and rules, could no longer be maintained. In modern times criticism of authority is the dominant motif of historical consciousness, in which reference to the historically conditioned nature of theoretical reasons and practical demands transmitted through institutions served to relativize them. This can then be interpreted as the motif of freedom. This sort of criticism of authority has proven fruitful everywhere and has not lost any of its contemporary relevance. But today it no longer demands any particular intellectual effort. On the contrary, it is now one of the features of contemporary scholarship that is conditioned by tradition, and to whose validity one can appeal as something that is taken for granted. Therefore it is particularly important to cast light on the "historically conditioned nature of the ethical consciousness" in its specifically ethical meaning and not to use it for denunciation of that consciousness.

When W. Pannenberg (*Wissenschaftstheorie und Theologie*, 1973, p. 412 [*Theology and the Philosophy of Science*, 1976]) in this connection stresses the historical nature of Christianity itself, it is his intention to make this historical nature determinative for ethics in the sense of a framework in which "the theme of the religious meaning of humanity is seen as the true basis for ethics." In his view this is mediated by the "contemporary understanding of truth." Criticism is only the preparation for constructive work and thus cannot be regarded as absolute.

The meaning of "criticism" in the framework of an academic concern for ethics must be specified in another aspect as well. Within theology the concept must primarily be clarified for theologians. Ethics has its scholarly place within the realm of the study of academic theology. We must inquire into the function of such academic study for theologians who are the pastors of churches and teachers of religion. The answer would then be that the academic study of theology in all its subdisciplines should aid theologians as future pastors and teachers in the formation of an identity that transcends their identity as individuals. The goal of an academic education is formation of a professional attitude which enables pastors in the practice of their profession to associate not only with their peers, that is those who have a similar religious and social background, but also with highly different persons under widely varying circumstances. Academic study should therefore enable pastors to maintain a critical relationship to themselves, that is, an identity that transcends their personal identity and enables them to view the world from standpoints other than their own. Academic study can and should contribute to that identity by enabling them to step outside their own egocentric position and in a scholarly manner enter into debate with the widest possible variety of themes that have relevance for the church and for Christianity. In this constructive sense the critical meaning of academic scholarship cannot be attained without the ethos of the scientific attitude, which consists in being critical not only and not primarily of "others," but of one's own standpoint. This ethos of the scientific attitude must be regarded as the most important element in the pursuit of academic study.

It is also necessary to speak of an ethos of ethics in its critical aspect in another respect. If it is true that a theoretical concern for ethics itself is a component of a permanent ethical discourse which is carried on in the realities of human life, then within theology ethics must also develop a consciousness of that discourse as it is continuously carried on in the church and in the Christian community. The theologian as ethicist is not the final authority for Christian ethics and should not pose as such. In the church and the Christian community, by means of the institution and individual life of the church and the community, much ethical work is done which in its own way has bearing for the ethical meaning of this activity.

It would be a different and far-reaching undertaking to single out and describe the ways by which ethical judgments are arrived at in the church and the Christian community. To mention only one especially conspicuous example, the well organized efforts of the Evangelical Church in Germany to deal with ethical problems have found expression in a multiplicity of study documents and pronouncements that are worked out by task forces appointed for that purpose. This practice of itself led to a recognition of the need for an evaluation of the conditions for and possibility of church ethics. See the "Denkschrift über die Denkschriften": *Aufgaben und Grenzen kirchlicher Äusserungen zu gesellschaftlichen Fragen. Eine Denkschrift der Kammer für soziale Ordnung der Evangelischen Kirche in Deutschland,* 1971. ("Study Document on Study Documents": The Task and the Boundaries of Church Pronouncements on Social Questions. A Study Document of the Commission for Social Order of the Evangelical Church in Germany, 1971.)

We can expect that scholarly ethics will endeavor to show how its basic elements and its methodology can be translated into a concrete ethic (Part Four). But it would be inappropriate to expect a set of "recipes" and to try to turn the ethicist into a sort of Protestant Chair of St. Peter. Concrete ethical statements are concrete expressions of ethical argumentation in reference to specific issues of life, which do not constitute the raw material that is to be made accessible to ethical theory; rather they constitute the reality of life that occasions and demands moral discourse. Thus the ethos of ethics must be preserved especially in reference to the concrete statements of ethics, in order to lead to a free discussion of the ethically relevant questions and so to aid in the taking of positions that are demanded by life in concrete situations.

PART TWO

THE THREE BASIC ELEMENTS OF
THE ETHICAL REALITY OF LIFE

What is it that an ethical theology investigates? To what is it related? With what does it concern itself? In a certain sense the answer to these questions is already given by the ethical reality of life. Ethics, as the theory of how life should be conducted, must be accountable for the presuppositions on which it is based and the manner in which it deals with these presuppositions. This part of our book will present the basic elements of the ethical reality of life, the perception of which constitutes the task of an ethical theology.

These basic elements are elementary in nature and form the basis on which the ethical task is analyzed in detail. The three basic elements of the ethical life that form the starting point of this study are first, *the givenness of life*, which must be taken into account in every action; second, *the responsibility of giving life*, which is encountered as basic to the structure of every action; and third, *reflection on life*, which determines and motivates the ethical consciousness.

The detailed analysis of these three elements must show to what extent they exhaust the task of an ethical theology. The systematic manner in which this will be pursued follows observations which are as precise as possible and which have basic significance for any understanding of the conduct of life. The analysis must show the relationship of the three basic elements of each other and how they are related to the line of theological thought followed here.

The discussions in Part Two are oriented both in content and in structure toward the themes which will be developed in detail in the methodology of ethics (Part Three) and in debate with the various approaches to ethics.

1. The First Basic Element: The Givenness of Life

a. The Givenness of Life as the Basic Situation of Ethics

The problems and tasks of life arise only for a life that is given. The givenness of life is the elementary presupposition that must be taken into account in every concrete, specific action. Through the knowledge of this elementary feature of all conduct of life, the reflective nature of ethical thought finds its initial, fundamental meaning.

This knowledge takes on ethical form when it is expressed as the statement that *no person can give life to him or her self.* There is no exception to this givenness of life. Therefore as our starting point it is anything else but trivial as soon as it claims its place in the consciousness of human activity. Only within the boundaries of the life that is given to a human being can an action be a specific accomplishment in concrete responsibility. Therefore the conduct of life as the living out of the life history of an individual is the context in which ethical reflection takes place. The ethical theme of the conduct of one's life is not everything that might possibly be done; it is that for which a single given life can be responsible. This by no means implies a limitation of the ethical imagination. On the contrary, this gives scope to the fact that all sense of desire and duty is mediated through the givenness of life. Only through such mediation does it take on an ethical quality. It is because human beings have to assume responsibility for the concrete reality of their lives that all desire and duty receives its specifically ethical quality. The basis of ethics is not constituted by timeless norms and laws of conduct that are superior to life. Norms and laws signify first of all that the life of each person, his or her life story, is part of a context in which the reality of life transcends the individual. Thus we are not pleading here for an "individualistic" ethic, but for a biographical ethic that is oriented to the conduct of life. Ethics as the theory of human living must at the outset and at every point of its development make sure of its empirical, experience-based fundamentals which are the raw material for ethical reflection.

Therefore the givenness of life is a basic assumption not only for the individual, but also for groups, societies, systems of historical communities, and periods of history. The first step in the perception of the ethical task is not an arbitrary control over possible courses of action, but the exploration of situations in which actions will be taken and the consciousness of the presuppositions for action. To this extent the givenness of life can be termed the *basic situation of ethics*.

Dietrich Bonhoeffer formulated the basic ethical situation as follows: "The question of the good encounters us always in a situation which cannot be undone retroactively — we are living. In any case, this means that we can no longer pose the question of the good, or answer it, as if our first task were to create life beautiful and good." "Not what is good in itself, but what is good under the presupposition of the givenness of life and for us — that is our question." "The question of the good is a part of our life, just as our life is a part of the question of the good" (E. Bethge, ed., *Ethik*, Munich, 1953, p. 166).

Here we touch on a central question of recent ethical debate that is usually framed in terms of two alternatives, normative ethics or situation ethics. In its debate with a normative ethic that seeks to develop the basic criteria of ethics from a general normative standard of conduct, unconditioned by time, situation ethics directs our attention to the specific demands which in each concrete situation must be perceived in new ways, specific to that situation.

W. Korff made an extensive study of the concept of normativeness during which he developed, in contrast to the historical nature of specific norms, the fact of their "non-arbitrary nature," which he derived from the "basic feature of reason, that is, to strive for freedom from contradiction." Korff brought a "historical" non-arbitrariness and a "natural" non-arbitrariness of human normative thinking into a relationship to each other such that normative ethics and situation ethics no longer appeared as alternatives, at least not on this quite basic level. *Norm und Sittlichkeit. Untersuchungen zur Logik der normativen Vernunft*, 1973, pp. 62ff.; 76ff. Korff arrived at conclusions that agree completely with the understanding of the basic situation of ethics developed in this present book. Cf. Korff, *Theologische Ethik. Eine Einführung*, 1975.

The critical interest which J. Fletcher's *Situation Ethics*, 1966, takes in the individual nature of each action is directed against an understanding of norms that is hostile to life and is to be enforced without consideration of the situation. This concern can be appropriated in that it aids in establishing

the basic situation of ethics. The German edition of Fletcher's book was published under the misleading title, *Moral ohne Normen?* ("Morality without
Norms?"). P. Lehmann developed a situation ethic in the fundamental ethics
sense intended here: P. Lehmann, *Ethics in a Christian Context,* 1963.

The impression that these two approaches are alternatives vanishes
if we abandon the abstract concept that there is a changing line of
specific, context-free situations that demand action. The obligatory,
situation-specific nature of human action is, rather, the result of the
basic situation of all action. It has been specified here as the givenness
of life, which as such constitutes the norm for all special situations.
This then indicates the content and method of ethical reflection.

Karl Barth in his *Church Dogmatics* made extensive use of the
easily remembered formula, "a human being exists through actions."
This formula says that action, more than anything else, implies
taking a position in reference to the reality of one's own life. But the
formula is so close to the equating of action and living fully that it
can be misleading. It follows from our formulation that no one gives
himself life that no one exists through his own actions. A person lives
actually and concretely through actions. But before life can be realized through carrying out action, life must first be given to the
person.

We will now ask how this first qualification of the basic structure
of ethics can be further differentiated and developed.

b. The Receiving of Life

If the statement, no one can give himself or herself life, is reformu-
lated in terms of an action, it would read "a human being must
receive life." This second element is an intensification of the perception of the basic state of affairs from which we started. In view of the
conditions under which the present discussion of the bases of ethics
is carried out, it is an element that needs clarification. It includes a
critique of the basic assumption in the popular view that the only
truly free human being is one whose life is not dependent on anyone
else. This assumption can turn into the pathos of human "self-
production" which discloses that the given interest in self-realization
points the way to unlimited obligation. But that is not really a constructive thought. For its realization requires the negation of the fact
that a human must first receive life before being able to lead his or
her own life. This negation, however, would have to deny something
that cannot be denied. As a result the negation leads to a practical

struggle against the basic situation of one's own life as a life that has been received. This can take the form of the struggle of children against their parents, of subjects of a society against that society's structures, and so forth. In every instance, however, it necessarily falls short of the goal that has been set, simply because of the logic that a life that has been received can never negate itself for the sake of constituting itself. Consequently this view tends to seek solutions through criticizing everything that exists, simply because it is given. This second basic element is relevant as an explanation because it calls attention to the activity that already takes place in the reception of life. The received life is not identical with biological existence. Life that realizes itself through the process of being lived is life that has been received and thus it assumes elementary responsibilities and unavoidable challenges. Each human being must receive life, that is, a person in this basic situation is not in a situation where it is first of all possible to weigh the decision whether or not to receive life, and if so when and how to give a beginning to one's own life. The impulse and motivation to act, the conduct of life, are not the result of reflection over dispositions that place one at the disposal of one's own self. A human being must receive life, that is to say, as an ethical agent, as a human who is called and challenged to lead life, that person's life is something given. That life which a human being receives is a life destined to be led in its own way. This constitutes an elementary responsibility. Whatever may come to be recognized in one's ethical consciousness as duty and may be encountered in various ways in changing inner situations in life, derives its inner obligatory nature from the structural challenge of the received life itself. This involves an understanding of the situation fundamental to ethics — that an active human life as action in relationship to others and to the surrounding world is a consequence of the fact that life is something received. This situation is expressed in the old idea that life is a calling, that one has a life calling. This concept lets us understand the conduct of life as a task that is included in the received life itself. It is the condition for the possibility that human beings generally are receptive for that which constitutes the content and intention of moral laws and commands.

In contemporary Catholic moral theology the question of elementary ethical responsibilities has been approached in a new manner in that the Catholic natural law tradition has entered into debate with the modern understanding of freedom, and thus seeks also to win for itself a basis for responsibilities that take precedence over the concept of autonomy. In this respect the interest in fundamental theology is, in its ethical consequences, quite close to the approach taken here, even though markedly different phases in the debate can be observed. See especially A. Auer, *Der Mensch hat Recht. Naturrecht auf dem Hintergrund des Heute*, 1956, and *Autonome Moral und christlicher Glaube*, 1971; F. Böckle, *Fundamentalmoral*, 1977 [*Fundamental Concepts of Moral Theology*, 1968]. On the debate, cf. B. Stoeckle, *Grenzen der autonomen Moral*, 1974.

c. The Elementary Freedom of the Individual Life

Since one of the givens of life is that it has been received there are basic responsibilities that modify in specific ways the positions which an individual can take. These responsibilities can be summarized as the dependence and the freedom of a life that is not the result of a person's own will. Everything that is or can become the theme and content of the conduct of human life depends on the givenness of life. That is to say, the actual living out of one's life depends upon abilities that have been given. Therefore the ethical theory of the conduct of life requires a clear understanding of the positive meaning of dependence. The theory cannot start from the assumption of an unlimited capacity for action by the individual, a capacity which is only later limited by the necessity of living together with other persons. This concept of a general capacity for action is abstract as long as it assumes that the coexistence of one's own life with the lives of others is a limitation subsequently imposed on the individual's own unlimited competence. Such a concept of a merely secondary limitation of one's possible courses of action because of consideration of others makes mutual dependence in the activities of life seem to be a task that must be performed at the cost of freedom, however good the reasons for it may be. If this were so, dependence would not be a feature of the ethical reality of life, but merely a limitation imposed from outside, even though imposed by reasons of expediency. The concept of dependence, however, should include as a productive component of basic reflection the fact that the reality of an individual's life is always conditioned and that everyone is and remains dependent on others. This is the inherently social nature of human life. Living ethically gives form to this dependence, and in the knowledge of this inherent social conditioning it is possible to regard as freedom even that dependence of a life that we owe to others.

This specific nature of a life owed to others constitutes the reality of individual freedom. For a person does not receive life in general but receives his or her own life. It can be distinguished from the lives of others by the elementary fact that only one person can live that particular life. No one can substitute for you in the living of your life. Even though there are occasions where one person can act for another, this is possible only for specific, limited functions. In the most basic sense then, one's own life is free, because in its individuality it can be lived only by the specific person to whom it is given. In addition, an individual life must be regarded as free because in terms of humanity as the totality of human life, any individual is unnecessary. In relation to the empirical totality of "all" humans, an individual life is contingent and unnecessary. It is not necessary for "me" to exist in order for humanity to exist. But this holds for each individual and thus for all. Freedom is therefore contingent on the empirical reality of one's own life, and the living of one's own life is by its very nature independent and must be carried out by the individual himself or herself. In this sense it is also the precondition of all social relationships. Consequently it is correct and proper for ethical theory to include criticism of any form of political, social, or moral conduct of life that does not take into account the freedom of the individual.

This third element of a derived and therefore free life constitutes the basis on which the historical living out of one's life is a permanent *individual expression* of the reality of life. Thus this concept of individuality will later (Part Four) play a role in the methodological approach to the "Concrete Issues of Ethics." Its relevance for the contents of ethics is that a truly human structure of the world cannot determine or prescribe from the outside in an abstract way the possibilities for living and thus rob the individual of his or her own life. A truly human structure of the world must be one which is realized through the individual's own conduct of life, and to that extent is based on freedom. Such freedom, however, does not mean absolute autonomy, but the freedom of a derived and received life, the freedom of the reality of individual life.

This brings us to a further aspect of the first basic element of ethics.

d. The Acceptance of One's Own Life

The individual must accept the life that he or she has received. This statement expands the elementary and basic structure of ethics, because it includes taking a position in relationship to one's own life and therefore the concrete task of ethical reflection on that life. Taking a position toward one's own life is an elementary ethical demand that involves the structure of one's identity.

A significant stimulus to recent discussions of identity was provided by G. H. Mead, *Mind, Self and Society*, 1965; E. H. Erikson, *Identität und Lebenszyklus*, 1970. An impressive and informative survey of the consequences for ethics was provided by H. Ringeling, "Das Problem der Identität," in *Handbuch der christlichen Ethik*, vol. 1, pp. 474ff. The identity of the individual as an ethical subject is not something that is given unmediated or naturally or that is simply to be protected and preserved against external influences. Such an understanding of identity would not include the ethical task but would lead to a strategy of pure non-involvement. Instead, identity involves a task, the demand that a position be taken toward one's own life. In all activity the question of the identity of the individual is a major theme, because it is the distinction between life in general and one's own life that sets the theme. Here we must bear in mind the thesis (p. 17 above) that ethics is more than a theory of action, because the conduct of human life involves more than actions.

In this connection see the criticism brought by W. Pannenberg against the dominance of sociological theories of action in *Wissenschaftstheorie und Theologie*, 1973, pp. 82ff., especially his criticism of J. Habermas on pp. 100ff. [*Theology and the Philosophy of Science*, 1976, pp. 80ff. and 98ff.]. Pannenberg's thesis that theories of action are dependent on prior interpretations can be defended against the objection that it is merely an opinion only if his thesis can be shown to be necessary to the structure of activity itself.

The status of the discussion of the concept of identity can be documented in its breadth and diversity. See O. Marquard and K. H. Stierle, eds., *Identität* (Poetik und Hermeneutik VIII), 1979.

In elementary form, a position is taken toward one's own life in relation to life in general wherever we raise such questions as, Why am I who I am and not someone else? Why am I male and not female? I would rather be blond and beautiful instead of brunette and merely pretty. I would rather be someone else, or, in intensified form, I would like to be who I am and someone else too, that is, everything that is humanly possible. The issue is simply that it seems possible to refuse to be who one is, or at least to try to be someone else. This attempt to lead another life, or to lead life in general is found in many nuances and in unending variation in all situations where action is taken, and it gives rise to a permanent uneasiness and readiness for change in the background of human relationships. It also appears frequently and explicitly in the foreground of social and political debates, for example, in demands that the actual situations of life must be open to the possibility of self-realization in every direction. Taking a position toward one's own life, recognizing the necessity of accepting life, is the essential theme of living, the heart of human biography. But this taking of a position acquires ethical form only when through reflective thought one becomes aware of his or her task. The distinction between one's own life and life in general means for ethics neither that a human being is simply identical with that which he or she is by nature or prior history (the natural misunderstanding), nor that the person has his or her identity in the possibility of becoming everything that he or she desires (the voluntaristic misunderstanding). This distinction means that an individual's task in life in general, and thus also in company with other humans in a society that transcends the individual, can be comprehended only in one's own, specific, individual manner. Each human being must come to self-acceptance as a specific individual. The distinction is basic to the concept of ethical responsibility. It is, however, a distinction within a relationship, not the separation of one's own life from life in general.

In a final aspect, we will now consider specifically the theological dimension of the basic structure of ethics.

e. Humanity as God's Creation

All the elements of givenness of life are brought together in an understanding of humanity as created by God. The theological formulation of this basic structure must therefore gather up the previously mentioned elements and discuss why it is that religion — the expression of the relationship of humans to God — is an ethically relevant basic dimension of the conduct of human life.

1) The Theological Significance of Life as Given

The inner context of the basic elements of ethics can be expressed, for example, in the terms of the first article of Martin Luther's "Small Catechism," "I believe that God has created me and all that exists" (text in *The Book of Concord: The Confessions of the Evangelical Lutheran Church*, trans. and ed. by T. G. Tappert [Philadelphia: Fortress Press, 1959], p. 345).

A correlation of the basic elements of the givenness of life developed above and Luther's statement results in the following picture.

The statement "no one can give life to himself or herself" has its theological counterpart in the confession of "God" as the creator of life.

The statement "a human being must receive life" corresponds to the confessional statement's "created," that is, the acknowledgement of creatureliness.

The statement "the givenness of life has its elementary responsibility in the relationship of the dependence and freedom in the reality of one's own individual life" finds its depth of theological and religious dimension in the confession that God has created "me."

The statement "the life that has been received must be accepted by the individual" is reflected in the confessional statement, "I believe," insofar as faith gives expression to an attitude of trust and of being accepted, something that includes the conditioned nature of my own life, over which I have no control, and yet which I must accept.

Through such a correlation of the confessional statement and the basic elements that were worked out in the discussion of ethical reflection on the reality of life we are able to see the theological significance of those elements. The theological theme is that we cannot avoid the question posed by life itself. It involves the question that is unavoidable for every ethic which has concrete expression as its goal: How are we to conceive of responsibility in relation to life in general at the point of a specific individual life and its conduct? Its goal is the discovery of the bases on which a responsible attitude to the reality of life is also the question of the reality which is the basis and the support for human life. Thus it is the question of the "ought" within the "is," of the fundamental theology which is immanent in ethics, or the question, To what extent can the statement that a human being is God's creature serve as a basic ethical premise?

In the context of the doctrine of creation, G. Ebeling begins with the relationship of faith and life. "The discussion of faith begins with the question of its relationship to life" (*Dogmatik des christlichen Glaubens* I, 1979, pp. 79ff.).

This question arises whenever a distinction is made between a specific individual life and life in general, in the form of taking a stand or confronting an ethical imperative. Here the nature of ethics as reflection comes to the fore. For instance, What does the statement that a specific life has come from God mean today in the light of the obvious fact that it has come from the individual's parents? The theological perception of this fact (which can be reduced to the merely biological) is that in every case one is responsible for his or her own life, independent of that life's specific and distinctive origin. Life as something given is independent of the specific manner in which it came to be, for example, through my parents or my socialization, or through the influence of history and society. This is the starting point for the realization that there is specific, concrete, ethical responsibility. Independence is not seen as a binding obligation until it can be said that life, whatever else can be said about its origin, is given by God. Thus a life that has come to birth, in spite of all dependence on such things as the decision of the parents to conceive and bear a child, and the quality of this decision, it is still independent, it is still one's own life. In the context of the specific life it is necessary to reaffirm life as such beyond its specific historical and biological origin and to take a stand toward life. This necessity is a fact of life, because in any case one must live one's own life, and through one's actions realize the relationship of one's individual life to life in general.

Suppose that in reference to one's specific life one feels impelled to cry out, "I wish I had never been born!" (cf. Job 9:21). Because this cry expresses the wish that life were over, it is related to that specific life which brought forth this cry of distress. What the cry really means is "I don't want to live this way; I want to live differently." The specific life, where it is not accepted, appeals to life in general, that is, it goes behind its own specific reality, its own individuality. Rejection of a specific life does not release one from the necessity of affirming life, since that rejection is possible and real only because there is a life that has been given.

2) Creatureliness and Freedom

If we examine human creatureliness in terms of the relationship to life which this implies, it is clear that the concept of creatureliness involves a relationship to the subject of all reality, the Creator. Speaking of human creatureliness involves speaking of the basic elements of theology. In a certain sense the essential statements of Christian theology can be regarded as a new approach to human creatureliness. This is especially true of the Christian concept of freedom as the central concept of Protestant theology and ethics.

For example, the meaning of freedom is made clear in Karl Barth's discussion of ethics at the beginning of his doctrine of creation as a broadly based doctrine of freedom. *Kirchliche Dogmatik* III, 4, 1958. See also Barth, *Das*

Geschenk der Freiheit. Eine Grundlegung evangelischer Ethik, 1953. E. Hirsch makes the pointed statement, "It is not possible to think of Reformation Christianity without unconditional Christian freedom; to do so would be to destroy it completely" (*Das Wesen des reformatorischen Christentums,* 1963, p. 114). Compare further R. Bultmann's understanding of freedom in "Gnade und Freiheit," 1948, and "Die Bedeutung des Gedankens der Freiheit für die abendländische Kultur." Both are found in *Glaube und Verstehen* 2, 1952, pp. 149ff., 274ff. In his ongoing debate with the modern concept of autonomy F. Gogarten developed his theological understanding of freedom. See the summary of his argument in *Die Wirklichkeit des Glaubens,* 1957, pp. 44f. See also W. Trillhaas, *Die christliche Freiheitsidee. Akademische Reden,* 1952, pp. 5ff. E. Jüngel's judgment is close to the truth: "If present day theology has any central theme it is that of Christian freedom" (*Zur Freiheit eines Christenmenschen,* 1978, p. 16). In this connection there is always interest in the relationship between a theological understanding of freedom and the various modern concepts of freedom, a relationship that can be expressed in a variety of ways. See for example O. Bayer, "Zum Ansatz theologischer Ethik als Freiheitsethik," in ZEE 17 (1973): 145ff; J. Baur, *Freiheit und Emanzipation,* 1976.

When we ask what is the logical relevance of the ethical argument, we are asking why humans have ethical insights in the first place, insights encountered in the reality of life. Ethical questions, as questions which humans ask about themselves, have as their theme the creaturely nature of humanity, and thus the relationship of the creation to its Creator. Humanity as the creation of God is the humanity that God desires, that is, humanity that sees its full and true destiny as its true nature. The identity of humanity as God's creation, which involves the question which humans ask concerning themselves, arises in this context. In this identity humans are free, if freedom can be defined as a life in harmony with oneself. Freedom in a theological sense then is the reality of one's own life in correspondence to God's intention as Creator. This freedom is the challenge confronting humans in the living out of their own lives.

On the theological understanding of the concept of person, see W. Pannenberg, "Person und Subjekt," in O. Marquard and K. Stierle, eds., *Identität,* 1979, 407ff.; and Pannenberg, *Gottesgedanke und menschliche Freiheit,* 1972, esp. pp. 44ff.

This relationship enables us to distinguish between human beings and the world in which they live. Personhood is a basic aspect of human dignity. The Christian concept of freedom involves the reali-

zation that a dependent and, in empirical terms, thoroughly misera-
ble humanity is a part of the reality of God's world. Personhood as
human individuality therefore does not mean a sum of properties
which a human being is in and of himself or herself. It does not consist in the ability to have control over oneself as over an object. Christianity preserves and transmits an awareness of the human dignity of
persons, who seen in themselves are thoroughly corruptible and
sinful. But even as such, each individual is inalterably in his or her
concrete personhood a creature of God. That statement does not
assign the person to a category, but refers to an individual, a contingent being with a personhood that is equivalent to the way we think
of God. Without this individual and at the same time contradictory
personality, an ethic involving reflective thought about the conduct
of life would be inconceivable. The personhood and individuality of
the concrete human being give expression to the significance of
creatureliness for freedom. They are prior to any activity involving
other humans. And therefore they constitute a boundary for all
activity, a standard for political, social, and moral programs for
structuring our world. The dignity and worth of the individual
person therefore is the basis for a defense of human beings against the
"world." That is to say, freedom can be defined as the limit on the
authority of one person over another. As a consequence of creaturely
freedom, this limit is an essential feature of each person's self-
limitation in relationships with others and in relation to the surrounding world.

In addition to individuality and personhood, therefore, a further
element in the concept of the freedom of created beings is socialization. The logic of ethics calls attention to the role of communication
in the structure of the reality of human life. No one can exist alone,
by and for himself or herself. Creatureliness as individuality and personhood has by its very nature a social dimension. The ethical significance of this dimension makes our relation to God explicit. It is
a relationship which is involved in the nature of humans as God's creation, in the mutual dependence of humans on one another, and in
their reciprocal relationship. This relationship expresses our consciousness of community with God in such a way that it makes us
aware that we all belong to the same world. Thus the elementary
norm for mutual recognition and acceptance of human beings in
their social relationships is love as the form of freedom, through
which they find themselves confronting their true nature.

In relationship to these basic structures of creatureliness freedom can then be defined in terms of the activity of the self (and thus not in terms of its nature!). The expression "activity of the self" affirms that the question of the real identity of the self is the theme of all human activity, and that therefore all activity is by its nature self-determination. The content of this self-determination must correspond to the basic relationships in which a human being is truly himself or herself. This is what is at issue in theological ethics. If the activity of the self as an element in freedom means that I am aware of myself in all my activities, it must also and more specifically mean that I am aware of the fact that I can be myself only in relation to God and to other human beings.

3) The Problem of Sin

Autonomous activity would be an empty term if its content were nothing more than a direct natural correspondence of a human being with that person's self, a correspondence that could be maintained in spite of all opposition to it and all negation of it. But here we must speak of activity in a quite specific context. This involves the elementary problem that in the concrete living of their lives human beings are capable of going against the reality of freedom, that their own activities fall short of achieving their destiny. This is the problem of sin.

Paul gave to Christian theology the idea that sin is not to be localized in an external transgression of the law (even though this understanding of it has remained alive), but in the difference between willing the good and being able to accomplish it (Rom. 7:13–25). Sin as the inability, even with the best of intentions, to do what is good expresses the insight that the human will cannot do what is good, if the will itself is not in accord with reality. The will cannot accomplish anything in and of itself, but only by working together with God, because God is the ground and goal of all reality, including human reality. For exegetical studies see E. Käsemann, An die Römer. Handbuch zum Neuen Testament, vol. 8a, 1973, pp. 189ff. The sharp distinction which Käsemann draws in his explanation of the concept of the ethical is, however, not convincing, because he is obviously working with a concept that was characteristic of dialectic theology, and which equates "ethics" with human ability as such (see p. 67). For another view see the exegesis of Paul's thought in U. Wilckens, "Was heisst bei Paulus: 'Aus Werken des Gesetzes wird kein Mensch gerecht'?", in Rechtfertigung als Freiheit, 1974, pp. 77f.

In a real sense it can be said that the distinctive approach of Christian ethics to the basic human question involves the problem of human sin and that it takes that problem as its specific theme. It accords a central place in the self-awareness of human beings to the difference between willing and bringing to accomplishment. And this has far-reaching consequences. It opens the way for a genuinely human participation in the reality of life, and does so where we see most clearly the problematic nature of the conduct of human life and of the manner in which humans construct their world. Thus the Christian understanding of ethics is not that it is merely the study of the good, and of the right way to live, but also and more comprehensively the study of human involvement with the whole of reality, and thus also with that which is the opposite of good, with sin, evil, contradiction and conflict. The readiness to include this side of life in the ethical question means specifically including human beings and human freedom. In this way human worth is taken seriously, and the relationship of ethics to reality is intensified. When the problem of sin is included in the quest of humanity for its true self, the negation of the good and the inability to accomplish it becomes an element of the human question. It ceases to be a question that is foreign and external to humanity, that reduces humanity to dependency, and becomes instead the question that is proper to humanity.

What it means to include this problem in the basic ethical question of what humanity is can be made clear by examining the alternative.

If we begin by assuming that to regard self-directed activity as freedom means that there is a direct correspondence between a human being and his or her true self, then all problems, all conflicts and shortcomings must be regarded as defects that prevent the individual from subjecting the world and others and making use of them in the manner that he or she desires. Instead of speaking of sin, we would then have to speak of an "evil" which confronts us in other individuals, the world, and society. The starting point for ethics then is not the reality of freedom but a situation of alienation and dependence. The goal of an ethical program would be the liberation of humans from such dependence. That would be ethics in the absence of freedom (on this issue see below, pp. 137–40).

A similar conclusion could be reached if autonomous activity were understood as one's ability at any time to make a new beginning. The only life or activity which could then be free would be one that recognized no presuppositions and began only with itself. On this understanding freedom would be characterized by the negation of the real relationships in which human life is lived. In a Christian life freedom as self-directed activity is clearly distinguished from this view. "Self-directed" as the equivalent of freedom means, in the Christian view, that working at the tasks set by the world, at the concrete duties and rights which constitute morality, is always at the same time working at developing one's self, performing actions in which the individual is directly involved. In this sense the goal of ethics is self-determination. This understanding of self-determination has given to Christian ethics and to the ethical culture shaped by Christianity a distinctive depth and intensity. The involvement of the self in ethical tasks and themes (as themes of one's own self-determination) is the inward standard of all undertakings and programs by which human beings relate to the world and to one another. All conceivable demands require personal involvement and personal responsibility and cannot be regarded as undertakings and programs on behalf of others. It is an inherent feature of the logic of Christian ethics that it cannot be enmeshed in casuistry, in a mass of specific instructions, commands and prohibitions, or in a catalog of specific Christian laws that portray a special area defined by the reality of the conduct of the Christian life. It is rather the nature of the logic of Christian ethics that it has as its theme the total range of the issues of human life.

Thus within Christianity the concept of freedom takes on the basic meaning of life in harmony with God as the Lord, that is, the one who is sovereign over all reality. God is also Lord of those dimensions of experience in which humans find that in their actions and attitudes they are in conflict with their nature as creatures. This is what it means to define Christian freedom in its essence as freedom from guilt and sin. This freedom is not found in the active fulfillment of laws and commands. It is to be found wherever the harmony of human beings with God is made possible as harmony with the one who is Lord of all that is required of us. That is the freedom we have in Christ.

Paul's Understanding of Christian Freedom

It is in this sense that in the New Testament Paul taught that freedom is a turning around made in the awareness of freedom. This turning is presented as the distinction between the letter of the law and the spirit of the demands of the law, as turning from the law that was given to Moses at Sinai to the new covenant which is based on faith in Christ. This understanding of freedom can be clarified by a paraphrase of several of Paul's basic statements.

In 2 Corinthians 3 Paul describes this new Christian concept of freedom by a metaphor which contrasts the letter of the law with the spirit of freedom. The climax of this contrast is found in v. 17: "Now the Lord is the Spirit, and where the Spirit of the Lord is, there is freedom." This spirit of freedom is the turning point for the new, Christian understanding of reality. Paul lays claim to it as the place where in the Israelite tradition God's law was given. That place is Mount Sinai, where the contents of the tables of the law, the Ten Commandments, were revealed to Moses. Sinai, the place where God's law was given, is the place of encounter with God the lawgiver. God is to be recognized and known in his law. After the exodus from Egypt the life which God gives was seen as life structured and determined by law.

But when Moses received the law on Mount Sinai and delivered it to the people of Israel, he had to place a veil over his face, because his face reflected the glory of God himself. For the message he brought was not about God himself as subject of all reality, but about God's law. But in Christ this veil is done away with. In him we encounter God himself. That is the point of the metaphor which describes the turning to an awareness of freedom.

Moses brought the law; that is to say, the teaching of the law became the way in which the reality of God was perceived and in which a life in harmony with God was to be led. But then our knowledge of God must be developed through a full knowledge of the law. The method of a religion of law is to define the law down to the most minute details for the conduct of life. Life was to be the living out of the instruction given in the law. This theological access to reality through the law was therefore determinative for the sociological structure of Israelite religion. The contents of the law and the instruction as to how to fulfill it bring God's law into play in principle at each point of the conduct of life, in small matters as well as in larger ones. What is required is to hold fast to the requirements of the law everywhere and in every matter. Knowledge of God's will can then be gained in the unending applications of the individual laws which are intended to determine how life is to be lived in all its details. This is the theological meaning of the law which leads to an intensification of the knowledge of the law.

This intensification is expressed in Paul's explanation by the concern over being required to fulfill all commands everywhere. Only by fulfilling the law in all its requirements can a human being be in accord with the reality of God. This concern for the law leads to dependence, to a loss of freedom. It is slavery to the law. The concern to be able to stand before God takes the form of the concern to keep the law everywhere, to fulfill all its demands. This concern keeps us from seeing God himself as the one who issues all these commands. The question of how to succeed in life, of how human beings are to be saved, is answered in terms of the law in the multitude of its requirements.

The turning point that leads to an awareness of freedom is reached when a person is dealing not only with the law or with God as the lawgiver, but with God himself, who is more than a lawgiver. God encounters his creatures as he the Creator intended to encounter them, as the one who wants to see human beings in full harmony with himself above and beyond humanity's success or failure in keeping the law. In Christ humans can know that they are accepted by God, without reliance on the law and its commands. This distinction between the law and the Spirit of Christ means that it is not the "letter" that makes us free, but the "Spirit."

This paraphrase of the conviction that we become aware of Christian freedom in turning away from Israel's understanding of the law shows that our insight into the bases for our actions can be gained when we see that our union with the one who commands, our community with God, is the foundation on which we are to live our lives. That is the content of Christian freedom. Humans are free, not in their own ability to carry out the specifications of the law but "in Christ." This awareness of freedom constitutes the distinctive sociological structure of Christianity, and it has attained importance in modern Christianity to the extent to which the human understanding of reality has been aware of its relationship to the one who is Lord. This distinction between "letter" and "Spirit" establishes the freedom we have in the activity we are commanded to perform, and combines the question of the meaning of one's own life with the question of the meaning of the law in such a manner as to give to ethics a deeper dimension of reality. Consequently, human activity has its starting point in a specifically defined life setting.

The foregoing argument for the basis of ethics would be inadequate if it were not continued in a specific development of the themes of human activity. The argument has reached the point at which it becomes necessary for the individual to desire a world in which life is to be lived. Belief in God as the Creator of life applies also to the world in which we are to live this life. Therefore the basic structure of ethics must be carried beyond its pre-ethical meaning into the dimension in which it becomes the theme for the task which humans are to perform.

2. The Second Basic Element: The Giving of Life

Until now we have been considering the givenness of life as the basic situation of ethics. Now we must turn to the basic structure of the active life. The inner logic of ethics is derived from the givenness of life. Ethics is interested in human actions and in the structure of actions in the context of life as it is given to humans. This logical relevance of ethics must also play a prominent role in the approach to ethical discussion. By analogy to the terminology of the "givenness of life," we will now speak of the task of giving life in order to depict the activity of a life of action. This task is firmly embedded in each person's own life in that a life that has been given involves in its course the lives of others. We are not to live for ourselves, because no one can live solely for or by himself or herself. In the daily living of life each of us interacts with and influences the lives of others.

a. Contributing to the Life of Others

The first step in defining this basic structure more closely is to show that in every instance living one's own life is influenced by the claims of its effect on others and by the way this takes place. This giving of life is not dependent on an explicit decision to take an action that could be omitted. It is an unavoidable part of each person's own life. And each explicit decision to act must also be oriented to this unavoidable state of affairs. Leading one's own life involves participation in and sharing in the life of the world around us.

In leading one's own life, the first implicit qualification is the ethical demand that we conduct our lives for others. This is essentially what it means to do good. A person's life should be useful to others. It is this that gives an ethical quality to our acts. And this quality inheres in all the actions that are performed for others and for the common good. The empirical functions that are performed and perceived as a person actually lives for others are the place where the basic ethical demands of such a life are encountered in concrete form.

The functions performed in one's life in the world define the ethical demand as something that is not added on to life, but is encountered in life itself. Thus the world in which we live becomes real for us in as far as it is characterized as activity in a world for others.

This is the basic thought which has led to finding life for others in concrete form in the doing of good through the ordinances of life. The functional character of ordinances means that they place an individual in the midst of a life for others. It is this structural feature that is decisive, not a specific historical, sociological form of these ordinances. Through the usefulness by which life for others is measured, the ethical demand is drawn into the context of the givenness of life.

At this point it is necessary to draw a distinction that indicates explicit ethical reflection. If in the normative ethical nature of the structure of human activities themselves we perceive a basic requirement to live for others, we can then say that this requirement is encountered in two distinct forms, as an "inner" demand that agrees with the living of one's own life, and as an "outward" demand that is imposed on and influences the moral agent from outside.

We can speak of an "inner" command when the demand that life be lived for others is recognized by the individual on the same grounds on which he or she recognizes the givenness of one's life as a life that is owed to others. Through the affirmation of our own life as a life owed to others, our life is drawn into the service of the transpersonal goals of actions that involve doing good for the benefit of others.

An "outward" command is encountered as a law that is imposed when the demand to live for others is experienced as being in competition with achieving the goals of one's own life. Then the same basic ethical command is seen as obligatory and as something that goes counter to the immediate self-fulfillment of the individual. It is a demand that lays claim from without to be heeded and fulfilled. Then the demand is perceived as being in tension with one's own life interests. It confronts us as a demand that is contrary to our self-fulfillment. This is the basic ethical conflict that leads to the development of an explicitly ethical discussion.

In terms of the basic structure of ethics developed in the discussion of the first basic element, we may say that this conflict arises when the distinction is not recognized between one's own individual life and life in general, when the individual life is identified with life in general. Then life loses its individual significance. The individual seeks to subordinate to his or her own purposes the functions involved in life for the world and to use them to satisfy selfish interests.

If our discussion is to have ethical consistency, we must hold that the "inner" and "outward" form of the command have the same ethical significance, that is, of structuring one's life as a life for others. It may well be that this significance comes into play in opposition to human self-assertion, in a way that places demands and constraints on the individual. Indeed, life is also subject to the constraints of ethical norms, even when the human agent is not consciously in accord with them.

In the above discussion we have attempted to reconstruct the basic significance that Martin Luther gave to Protestant ethics. The Reformation polemic against pious works in all its various expressions made the point that good works fall short of the meaning of the good, because people do them for their own sake, for their own salvation, for their own self-realization. The true meaning of "good" works is found, on the contrary, in that they are performed for the sake of others, for the good of the neighbor.

b. The Presence of Others in One's Own Actions

What role is played by the presence of others in one's actions? The others are by no means to be regarded merely as the recipients of good deeds or deeds motivated by good intentions. Such a one-dimensional understanding of actions would not hold up under ethical scrutiny. Human activity by no means has at its disposal the means sufficient to bring about the fulfillment of the good as the highest good, that is, in the sense of the good due to all others, even when we attempt to achieve this fulfillment. The supreme error of a "good" moral consciousness may well be the unreflecting assurance that it knows exactly what contributes to the physical and spiritual welfare of others. The tendency to assume moral control over others misses the ethical significance of the structure of human acts and gives free rein to the will to make others conform to our own acts and our own intentions. An ethical qualification of activity as "contributing to life" must allow scope for the cooperation of others in the structuring of life. One's own conduct is subject to the requirement that it be placed in the service of the good. The good that is to be achieved in this way (and whose content must be clarified in the subsequent course of this discussion) is not a function of one's own activity, the good intentions of one's goals and intentions, but quite on the contrary, one's own conduct must be placed in the service of the good. The good must be defined as a part of the world in which we live, and it must provide room for the lives of others.

In practical terms, devotion to the good "of others" must be incorporated into one's own actions, if those actions are dependent on rules. Rules are an ethical qualification of activity that mediates between one's own actions and the life of those whom these actions involve and affect. We spoke above of functions or ordinances in which "life for others" can be expressed in concrete terms. The expression "rules" for conduct calls attention to reflective ethical thought that is implicit in the perception of functions and ordinances. Actions must be distinguishable from control over others, and their consequences must be amenable to ethical responsibility. Submission to rules for conduct anticipates the involvement of others in the world in which we live and draws the presence of others into the sphere of our own actions.

In answer to the question of what constitutes human vocation if it is not conceived in terms of the explicitly religious "vocation" of the "religious" (such as the monastic life or church vows, etc.), Martin Luther said, "But if I am not called, what am I then to do? Answer: How can it be possible for you not to be called? You will have your place in life. . . . Look, just as no one is without commands to obey and a calling to follow so too no one is without work that is to be done aright" (WA X, 1, pp. 308, 6ff.).

Keith Ward sees the dependence of actions on "moral rules" as a specific basis for Christian morality, in so far as these rules as absolute obligations, independently of their varying expressions, reflect the claim of reality that limits human autonomy, a claim which is based on the "Being of God" "To be moral is to respond emotionally, volitionally, and cognitively to the reality of God." (*The Divine Image. The Foundations of Christian Ethics*, 1976, pp. 8–11.). This aspect of rules as responses is to be seen as contained in the social nature of real actions.

In this context we must recall the distinction between an "inner" and an "outer" form of this demand. The "inner" form of the demand means that according to its structure all activity inevitably affects others. This structure is not merely the content of individual moral consciousness, but is the objective meaning of all actions, the material quality of the reality of one's own actions. So that the structure of an action may remain distinguishable from the varying subjective goals of the agent, the subjective intention must undergo ethical qualification. That is what it means to say that goals must anticipate the effect that an action may have on others.

This anticipation is tested and modified by being subject to the "external" form of the demand, in that activity is governed by rules. Rules of conduct are not mere formal "rules of thumb" that can be established arbitrarily. The expression "rules" must rather indicate that actions take place in a living community in which persons are dependent on one another. The content and ethical qualification of such rules, their validity, depends on what it is that forms the basis of the community and what are therefore the goals for actions that take responsibility for preserving life. If "living for others" means more than simply submissuion to others or subjugation by them then the decisive factor is that which gives meaning to the community. Therefore we must go a step further and speak of the inherent social nature of the structure of activity.

c. Trust as the Inner Meaning of Social Relationships

The world in which we live imposes on human actions an elementary responsibility, that of trust. Thus in the structure itself of our actions we encounter both dependence and freedom. Anyone who takes responsibility for a life has obligations for that life. The productive form of this dependence is trust. Trust is the inner meaning of relationship in society. If we ask what sort of action trust expects, the answer is, help in living. The concept of trust introduces into the conduct of one's life the point of contact between our actions and the lives which they affect.

Knud E. Løgstrup developed this insight quite effectively. He wrote of an "unvoiced demand" which is encountered in every relationship between persons. He termed this demand "voiceless" because it precedes all rational guides to action and all expressly formulated demands. This voiceless demand is the expression of trust. According to Løgstrup trust is the original relationship between persons. K. E. Løgstrup, *Die ethische Forderung*, 1959, and "Die spontanen Daseinsäuzserungen in ethischer, sprachlogischer und religionsphilosophischer Sicht," in ZEE 20 (1976): 25–34.

The presence of trust is implicit in human relationships. Trust shows that we are dependent on others, and that this is a part of life.

Of course this trust can be betrayed, but only because the expectation of it is present in every human relationship. What we basically expect from the actions of others is that they will do nothing evil to us or against us, but that they will do that which is helpful and useful. Meaningful action is dependent on this expectation of trust, and it must show that it is thus dependent. Trust is the "ought" in human relationships.

Løgstrup therefore includes trust among the "spontaneous expressions of our being." In his analysis of these expressions he brings together the ideas of human creatureliness and love. Trust is the elementary expectation that one human brings to the actions of another. Activity is therefore the recognition of and the reaction to trust.

But trust is a highly problematic and precarious dimension of life. Trust can be misplaced, disappointed, and abused. Therefore, here too ethical reflection must distinguish between an "inner" and an "outer" dimension of trust. In respect to the "inner" dimension of trust in our actions, we may say with Løgstrup that in trust we encounter once again the basic ethical situation. By means of trust it is implicit in autonomous human actions that a person can be responsible only for that which is first given, that is, the expectations that others have. Actions are not absolute but take place in the setting of a shared life in community. Trust confronts moral agents with the challenge of accepting two facts: that they have received a life that has been entrusted to them, and that they encounter the trust of others. Thus we appropriate to ourselves the expectations that others have in us. Our actions must be trustworthy. This challenge is always immanent in the reality of the actions we take. It is not merely some desirable supplement to them.

In this spirit N. Luhmann devoted a penetrating sociological analysis to the role trust plays in the context of social relationship. N. Luhmann, *Vertrauen*, 1968.

When we speak of an "outer" dimension of trust, we mean that our actions are our cooperation with a world that is worthy of trust. The individual nature of each person's life prevents us from simply relying on an unproblematic mechanism of self-fulfillment in the relationship between our expectation of trust and our actions. On the contrary, the human world must be so shaped as to take on a reliable structure. The concrete expectation of trust is that each person will receive what is that person's due. Thus trust is basically involved with justice, and justice is a concrete result of trust. Participation in a world that is worthy of our trust involves us in a course of action in which the basic concern is that trust be incorporated into law and not be merely dependent on the original personal relationship of men and women to one another. This indicates the necessity of our reflecting on the "outer" dimension of our expectation of trust. The structure of human society that corresponds to this basic meaning of trust is one of community under law. Law can thus be regarded as a form of this "outer" dimension.

This understanding enables us to see that the concept of basic human dignity is a first step toward the realization of the significance that our actions have for society. In the approach to ethics which we are developing here, the understanding of human rights does not go back to a natural law that humans possess in and of themselves and which is protected over against society as their personal possession. Instead it points to a more basic understanding of human rights, in which persons have expectations of the actions of others, which it is their right to expect to have fulfilled.

The conceptualization of human rights is today the object of various theories, and cannot be fully carried out in terms of its modern historical origin in the Western concept of freedom. On the concept of human rights and its history, the reader should consult G. Oestreich, *Die Idee der Menschenrechte*, 1963, and *Geschichte der Menschenrechte und Grundfreiheiten im Umriss*, 1968; R. Schnur, ed., *Zur Geschichte der Erklärung der Menschenrechte*, WdF XI, 1964. Highly informative for the current discussion are M. Honecker, *Das Recht des Menschen*, 1978; W. Huber and H. E. Tödt, *Menschenrechte*, 1977; J. Baur, ed., *Zum Thema Menschenrechte. Theologische Versuche und Entwürfe*, 1977.

In the present context it is sufficient to comment that the idea of human rights includes the responsibility of human beings to be concerned for one another's welfare if they are to be just to one another. This acknowledgement constitutes the inner and the outer norms for our actions. Voicing this requirement implies that this assumption is by no means obvious, but also includes the task of overcoming those things that stand in its way. This leads to the next step in our discussion.

d. Accepting Responsibility for Others

It is essential that we accept responsibility for the life of other persons. Thus we come now to the creative dimension of actions, because responsibility for the life of others includes the dimensions of estrangement, separation, conflict, and hostility between persons. The structure of activity itself implies an explicit position in reference to the evil that exists in human relationships. It has far-reaching consequences for the structure of an ethical system whether this necessity of taking a position in opposition to evil is accorded basic importance in ethics, or whether the problem is relegated to an incidental role at the margin of an ethical theory that is concerned only with the good and its realization.

The experience of evil is not an external feature of human activity; it occupies a place within the relationship of human beings to one another, specifically in the refusal of mutual recognition. Whatever else can and must be said on this subject, any definition of evil that has relevance for our actions must stress that evil is in essence the active rejection, expressed in our actions, of responsibility for one's own life as a life for others, as a commitment to life. Evil is the power with which the capability for action goes counter to the basic meaning of human action.

The experience of evil and the knowledge of evil always presuppose a knowledge of good and take that knowledge into account. An exhortation like that of Paul, "Overcome evil with good" (Rom. 12:21), appeals to such knowledge and has as its goal the renewal of the insight that all action takes place in the context of a life that is derived from others and that is therefore under obligation to others. A knowledge of good capable of bringing about such renewal is the precondition for our being able to speak of evil at all, and in particular to speak of it in a way that is relevant for our own actions. A consequence of the demand that we assume responsibility for the lives of others is that we must come to understand the factors which hinder us in fulfilling this responsibility. It can only be fulfilled, however, and those factors can only be identified if we keep in mind the meaning of a "good" life when we are dealing with evil. And a good life is one in which the capability for action is in harmony with the basic meaning of human activity. Creative activity therefore moves toward a renewal of its original meaning.

The first question is then how we can interpret evil so as to develop its ethical significance in a way that will be relevant for actions. Kant held that quite simply and directly a person of good intention encountered evil "when among other persons" (*Die Religion innerhalb der Grenzen der blossen Vernunft*, vol. IV, preface, ed. W.

Weischedel, pp. 751–52). According to this view society is the locus of evil in the world. "It is sufficient that they (i.e., others) are there, that they surround a person, and that they are human beings, for them mutually to corrupt one another in their moral situation, to make one another evil." Kant's position, which has always caused his interpreters difficulties, arouses doubts, however, as to whether he has found the correct starting point. This starting point could lead to the conclusion that "humans" are good, but "others," or "the world" prevents them from doing what is good.

Can we then imagine a solution to this basic conflict that would consist in doing away with the "others" in order to make it possible to live in accord with the good? This direct morality of assertion of one's own intention to do the good, is widely practiced today in personal, social, and political discussions and debates. It can be seen particularly in the tendency to portray "others," or "society," as the site and focus of evil, in order to assert one's own goodness. Being good then means fighting against evil, that is, against "others," and in this struggle against evil, to strive to achieve good for oneself in opposition to the "others."

Doubts arise about this solution, however, because it ignores the fact that the "others" are an essential feature of the meaning of the actions that we take in our own lives, and therefore cannot be adduced later as disruptive factors in our efforts to live a good life. If this is ignored, then the morality of self-assertion, of insisting on one's own will to do the good, can become the supreme form in which evil is present among human beings. And responsibility for the life of others no longer plays a central role in our understanding of the good.

Among the historical consequences of this dichotomy, it seems to me, is also the formula which Reinhold Niebuhr used to express the basic conflict of ethical theory, *Moral Man and Immoral Society*, 1932.

An ethical theory that is relevant for ethical activity cannot begin with the struggle against evil, but must start with an understanding of evil itself, so that in this basic conflict the theory can be shown to be permeated by a knowledge of the good.

The first and most important step that ethical theology must take in this connection is the overcoming of evil through the acknowledgement of one's own guilt. The concept of guilt in Christianity expresses the insight that human beings owe life itself to one another and to God. Therefore the acknowledgement of guilt does not thrust persons into total impotence in the face of a reality that is in every instance dominated by evil, or paralyze them into total passivity. The acknowledgement of guilt also frees us from the attempt to wage the battle against evil from the position that one's own life is in principle superior and good. That acknowledgement involves and deeply affects the meaning of the empirical issues of how we live.

The transformation of "evil" into human "guilt" means that the experience of evil is incorporated into the basic social nature of one's own life, and that life cannot be lived for self alone. If the demand that we be responsible for the lives of others is the meaning of the reality of human actions, then evil is defined in terms of another point, namely a point within our own life, a life under obligation to others. The attempt to solve our basic conflict leads us then to a creative perception of our own life in the service of good.

We must now ask how the acknowledgement of guilt can be interpreted as a productive and creative process. That acknowledgement is possible only in relation to an instance which would derive a good and wholesome significance from such acknowledgement. Guilt in the sense of a guilty life can be formulated and identified only in terms of an instance in which that acknowledgement leads, not to the destruction of the individual, to the loss of that person's life, but to receiving forgiveness.

This is to say that when evil is ascribed to a human agent as that agent's own guilt, then in analogy to the approach set forth above, the consequence is that it is not "the others" who must be gotten rid of, but the "guilty" person. That person must be replaced by a good one. In this way the Reformation teaching of the "law that kills" could easily have fatal consequences. But this would be to ignore the fact that "guilt" in this profound sense is acknowledged not before human beings but before God. The acknowledgement of guilt is the anticipation of the forgiveness of guilt and therefore places the individual in a renewed relationship to God. Thus it follows that if the theological understanding of sin is consistent at this point, then a confession of sin implies the forgiveness of sin as the heart of the gospel. To this extent the good news of justification in reality and in terms of theology precedes the "law that kills." The productive and creative meaning of acknowledgement of guilt is expressed in forgiveness. In religious and theological terms, to accept life is to live through forgiveness.

That we have been forgiven means that our actions will be characterized by consideration for others. This is the creative meaning of the acknowledgement of guilt, and it is significant for everything we do. The acceptance of others should not be made dependent on whether they are just to us, acknowledge us, and help us in our life. An abstract demand for mutuality necessarily leads in cases of conflict and opposition to the result that the relations of persons to one another mark time and become fixed in mutual opposition. Considerateness overcomes this conflict, and is creative in that through the commitment of one's own life it brings about a new reality that overcomes the opposition. It goes beyond the existing situation, makes it merely relative, and enables it to change. As considerate action it goes beyond the standards of equality and of the equal worth of people, standards which can be used to attack others. Thus human actions, in their individual, representative nature become capable of being universalized because they move beyond abstract opposition and anticipate community through assuming responsibility for the life of others.

G. Sauter included guilt and reconciliation in the "constitution of community" and argued that they should therefore be removed from the semantic domain of juridical concepts. G. Sauter, "Versöhnung und Vergebung. Die Frage der Schuld im Horizont der Christologie," in EvTheol 36 (1976): 34ff, 39.

In reference to what has been said about the relationship of guilt and forgiveness to the solution of the problem of responsibility for the life of others, a distinction must be drawn between an "inner" and an "outer" form in which we encounter the demand to assume this responsibility. Thus far we have attempted to understand and explicate the "inner" structure of this demand. The theological arguments which we have used depend on the view that it is distinguishable from human self-forgiveness or self-redemption and remains so. In traditional theological terminology we can speak of the relationship between "Law and Gospel."

In the present century Karl Barth set in motion a renewed and vigorous discussion of the relationship of Law and Gospel. He stressed the idea that the Gospel is the factual and intellectual presupposition for the understanding of the Law and for the determination of its content (Evangelium and Gesetz, 1935). (This writing and the discussion it aroused are documented in the book edited by E. Kinder and K. Haendler, Gesetz und Evangelium, WdF CXLII, 1968.) I am in basic agreement with his position. But Barth's one-sided dogmatic development of this thought stresses the distinction between God and man, a distinction that gave rise to the problem in the first place. He does this so thoroughly in favor of God that the problem, for the sake of which the distinction between Law and Gospel was formulated, simply disappears.

There is significance in the distinction only if we hold strictly to the view that it involves the human subject and human conduct, and consequently must be worked out in detail through an ethical theology. Otherwise the result is that we deduce the ethical questions both "from above" and "downwards," and under the premise of the "verbum externum" of the Gospel there is no way to solve these conflicts that arise in life. The result among Barth's followers was a moralizing of Christology, which then led to new distinctions between "Christian" life and "human" life.

The Gospel of forgiveness as "verbum externum," as an external word, must be imparted to men and women. It makes them aware of the community of God with human beings, a community which includes human sin, and in which we can confidently trust for "external" encouragement. But this underlines once more that assuming responsibility for the life of others is not a supplementary act of the will, which is demanded of us above and beyond our own freedom and self-fulfillment. Rather it belongs to the reality of the new life that we receive from God.

The various formulations of a distinction between an "inner" and an "outer" form of the ethical demand represent the attempt to reformulate the traditional distinctions in the theological understanding of the law, which are now mostly taught to theology students in review for their examinations ("usus elenchticus legis," or "usus theologicus legis," or "usus civilis legis," etc.). These traditional distinctions are collected in H. Schmid, *Die Dogmatik der evangelisch-luterischen Kirche.* New edition, H. Pöhlmann, ed., 1978.

Paul Tillich described the overcoming of human alienation and conflict in a creative manner in his ontological analysis of love. I will give here only a brief summary as a commentary on my formulation, that "the acceptance of responsibility for the life of others anticipates community." Paul Tillich, *Liebe, Macht, Gerechtigkeit,* 1958 [*Love, Power, and Justice,* 1969]. Tillich termed love the "motive power of life," "being in actuality." Love, he said, is the power which attracts all beings to other beings. Love is the drive toward the unity of that which is separated. Love enables us to think of the meaning of reconciliation, union, and reunion and at the same time, shows that separation is the separation of that which belongs together "by its very essence." To speak of the "power" of love means that separation does not have the same ontological status as unity. On the contrary, separation, contradictions among humans, presuppose an original unity. Unity, which must be identi-

fied in life itself, must be understood as encompassing both unity and separation. Thereby unity can be regarded as a reuniting. Our present life of unity
can be described as love, because love has as its theme unity in the situation
of separation. Love makes unity a present reality, as the original existence in
a situation of separation, and embraces separation on the basis of unity. Love
is the form of a relationship which is given even in separation or alienation.
Even alienation presupposes an original oneness. But love cannot be thought
of where absolute contradiction and absolute separation exist. From here Tillich comes to the thesis that life includes love as one of its constitutive elements. Tillich also includes within the ontological nature of love its
emotional nature, or its nature as feeling. Emotions and their motifs must
be explained in the light of the ontological character of love: the feeling of
love is the anticipation of a reuniting, and is contained in every human relationship. The ontologically based movement to others, to those from whom
we are separated, expresses itself by anticipation in our feelings. Thus it is
possible to speak of love as more than a "mere" feeling, to interpret the feelings or emotions as part of reality in ontological terms, and not to deny them
in the interests of love as the meaning of actions.

Compare to Tillich the study by E. Amelung, *Die Gestalt der Liebe*, 1972,
and for a full evaluation of Tillich's systematic contribution, see G. Wenz,
Subjekt und Sein. Zur inneren Entwicklung der Theologie Paul Tillichs,
1979, with an extensive bibliography on Tillich.

e. Love as the Form of Life in Freedom

By the concept of love ethical theology seeks to express the relationship between the receiving of life and the giving of life. The theological explication of the context seeks to show that love is an intensified
form of freedom. Love is not a scholarly term that takes its meaning
from a strictly theological derivation. On the contrary love is a word
that comes to us from everyday language and brings a rich variety of
meaning to ethical theory. This richness is also displayed in the bibli-
cal interpretation of the love commandment, as Jesus took it up and
gave it new relevance. It can be said of the basic command to love,
that love of one's neighbor summarizes the whole of the Law and the
Prophets (Matt. 22:38–39). In the meaning of this one word the relationship of humans to God is brought together with the relationship
of humans to one another. If we regard the love commandment as the
distinctive feature of Christian ethics, we must not understand it in
an exclusive, dogmatically defined manner. On the contrary, the concept of love has for the understanding of Christian ethics an inclusive
meaning that encompasses the basic elements of its experiences and
demands.

64

1) Love as an Intensified Form of Freedom:
On the Doctrine of Justification

What are the specifically theological arguments that come together in the understanding of the love commandment? First we must examine the reasons why the concept of love speaks in intensified and concise form of the freedom "for which Christ has set us free" (Gal. 5:1). This provides the theological basis for the answer which, following Paul and Reformation theology, runs as follows: Those who are free, who have been made free in Christ, do not act for their own sake, but for the sake of their neighbors. They act out of love alone. This answer includes as the indicative, the basis that has been worked out in the doctrine of justification.

"Justification" is a distinctive term of Protestant theology.

For a historical profile of the doctrine of justification, see the study of G. Müller, *Rechtfertigung*, 1977. Recent studies of importance for ethics include W. Lohff, "Rechtfertigung und Anthropologie," KuD 17 (1971): 225–43, and ed., *Rechtfertigung im neuzeitlichen Lebenszusammenhang*, 1974; E. Herms, "Die Kategorie der Rechtfertigung," in *Handbuch der christlichen Ethik*, vol. 1, 1978, pp. 422ff. In the following I will present a concise systematic reconstruction of the structure of the doctrine of justification and a paraphase of its elements that are relevant for actions.

The freedom which we have before God, that is, which is ultimately valid, is given to humans "without price," not as the result of human effort, but as the content of faith, or of one's relationship to God. It is given by God "for the sake of Christ." Faith is trust in Christ as trust in this freedom of justification. It sets humans free from the compulsion for self-realization. The christological basis of this freedom is that it has as its content the reality of community with God. That is the specifically theological meaning of love. "Christological" here means that God has committed himself to fellowship with humanity. God is not some abstract deity who abides beyond the world where humans dwell. Love is therefore a more precise definition of what we mean when in a Christian context we say, "God." Love as the concept which expresses God's fellowship with humanity is the condition under which the freedom that justification brings can be known as the fulfilling of the "law," that is, of the will of God. The inner meaning of the law is the realization of the community of men and women with God. The theological intention of the law is not made empty and meaningless by the love of God, but remains relevant in the realm of its fulfillment. Love is therefore also a more precious definition of life as a life "in God," that is, in trust in God and as the fellowship of humans with the subject of all the reality of life.

As a consequence of justification the purpose of human actions is to realize our fellowship with God as fellowship with one another. This realization is in accord with the christologically defined fulfillment of the law.

This line of thought was developed with especial clarity by Martin Luther in his tractate *De libertate Christiana,* 1520. Martin Rade rightly termed this writing "the first statement of the evangelical doctrine of faith" (in comparison with Melanchthon's *Loci* of 1521). Rade's magnificent discussion of this document is found in *Die Christliche Welt* 39 (1925): 2-3, 69-70, etc. E. Jüngel has also written a brief interpretation, *Zur Freiheit eines Christenmenschen,* 1978. What follows is my paraphrase of the argument in the final section of Luther's tractate.

The Christian is free from all works that have righteousness as their goal, and is now to serve other persons and to be useful to them. In this the Christian is to be like Christ. The activity of the Christian life is no longer based on the concepts of self-fulfillment, but is directed toward a restoration of fellowship with God, expressed in love. Just as our neighbor suffers and has need of us, so have we suffered in God's presence and are in need of his grace. Therefore just as God has freely helped us, so we, with our body and its works, that is, through the way we lead our life, should do nothing else than to help our neighbor. Fellowship with God and love for our neighbor are, according to Luther, two sides of the same reality, the same freedom. The Christian is not to live for self but for Christ and for the neighbor — for Christ through faith, and for the neighbor through love. And thereby in both these relationships the Christian abides in God's love. These elementary statements express the relationship between freedom and love, which we have described by saying that love is the form in which freedom is expressed in life.

2) The Relevance of Justification for Our Actions

The relevance of the doctrine of justification for action is an extremely critical point for ethical theology. Careful thought and reflection are needed if the theological motifs are to find expression in a manner that accords with reality. The concern in Paul's writings and in Reformation thought for the understanding of justification did not take the form of a supreme, general doctrinal statement from which all theology and ethics could be derived. Rather its starting point is in the midst of the reality of life as the point where we stand in relationship to God, and from there it confronts the basic questions of our understanding of reality. This finds expression in both method and content, because the discussion of justification in both systematics and history of doctrine is a part of Christology. The heart of the matter is the role of the human agent as ethical subject.

Thus it was easy for the discussion of the doctrine of justification in modern times to be oriented primarily toward the problem of the human agent as subject. This question draws together the reasons why Christian theology and ethics differ from any theory of the self-constitution of the human agents through their actions.

The line of argument may be stated as follows: If the nature of the human self were adequately defined by the self's own life of activity, then fulfilling one's own life would of necessity be the goal to which all other goals, including our relationship to God and to our neighbor, would be subordinated. Self-interest would then be the dominant guideline for action, and all other orientations would have to be subordinated to it. Our actions would be subject to the unlimited obligation to attain and accomplish that which constitutes our ultimately valid destiny.

The task of ethical theology to clarify the content of faith consists in disclosing that this attempt at ultimate vindication and self-fulfillment through our actions is a false path, full of contradictions. Ethical theology does this by unmasking the attempt as an alternative to the relationship of God to humanity. For in the duty of self-fulfillment the human agent is setting a task that no human can fulfill, because no human can in this way escape by thought or action from the relationship in which human life is being lived. Ultimately it must be acknowledged that it is our destiny to seek for self-realization in a relationship which is by its structure a theological relationship. The clarification of this situation is the inner, intellectual motif of the experience of faith, and gains its significance through leading us to the true meaning of our relationship to God.

Such an interpretation of justification can, in this modern period of autonomy, very quickly arrive at a critical point. The doctrine of justification in a certain sense makes human activity "purposeless," because one's own life is no longer a purpose in itself. From the point of view of the theological interpretation of the doctrine of justification as a doctrine of freedom, it is easy to conclude that the Christian is directly confronted by an "unworldliness" of faith.

This conclusion is drawn in a pointed and radical manner by R. Bultmann and F. Gogarten. For Bultmann's view, see his *Theology of the New Testament*, and for Gogarten's see *Der Mensch zwischen Gott und Welt*, 1952 and *Die Wirklichkeit des Glaubens*, 1957. Both expressed the theological concept that faith is not conditional on human activity. They left the human agent in a dilemma, however, in that the preservation of this unconditional nature became the only criterion for Christian action. The purity of faith as freedom from all empirical achievement thus became a way of incorporating ethics into the doctrine of faith. There then followed a characteristic argument that asked whether the necessary consequence would not be a non-ethic. A theory of action based on a non-ethic can be set forth only in such specifications that would permanently reaffirm the basic thesis that faith is "unworldly," subject to no worldly conditions, and as a result we would be confronted with the demand to let the world be the world.

Gogarten carried out this program in a highly interesting theology of secularization in his book *Verhängnis und Hoffnung der Neuzeit*, 1953. Here he gave systematic form to the theses of Ernest Troeltsch about the significance of Protestantism for the rise of the modern world (E. Troeltsch, *Die Bedeutung des Protestantismus für die Entstehung der modernen Welt*, 1911, reprinted 1963). For the relationship of Gogarten to Troeltsch see the work of H. Fischer, *Christlicher Glaube und Geschichte. Voraussetzungen und Folgen der Theologie Friedrich Gogartens*, 1967.

The problems characteristic of the work of Bultmann and Gogarten in ethics result from the same factors that led Karl Barth to characterize all ethics as the fall of man (see above p. 17).

This has resulted in a theological morass, the product of the particular confrontation in which the theological argument was developed. In this confrontation human self-discovery, human autonomy and self-realization became the sole dominant, negative theme of theology. As a result the makers of theological theories take on the basic characteristics of the position they are opposing. When anyone asserts that the unconditioned nature of freedom of belief is shown in the negation of autonomous human conduct, the whole theological argument is conceived solely from the standpoint of a self-determining human being. It thus remains mired in negation, and the Christian concept of freedom becomes a negative concept of modern autonomy. This also means the acceptance of the confusion of reality that theologians are convinced is involved in every program of unmediated self-fulfillment. As a result, no unbiased, liberated relationship to the ethical reality of life is achieved.

Ethical theology turns away from this theology of confrontation in

that it identifies the freedom of justification as residing in the individual, social, and historical reality of the life of empirical humanity,
and therefore finds relevance in the living out of life in its conditioned
nature.

The problems posed by making the doctrine of justification relevant to actions and decisions have their own tradition. Four dominant types of mistaken evaluations can be specified.

1. The antinomian error holds that the Christian is free from the
"Law" and can thus live out his or her individual freedom (in the
sense of an unmediated expression of one's own faith), and thus
the individual falls into a sort of higher libertinism. On the basis of
the insight that the "Law" no longer places any demands on our
lives the conclusion is drawn that there are no commandments
applicable to the freedom that comes from faith. This freedom is then
expressed in an individualistic manner. Freedom itself becomes the
goal, and the question of the relationships in which that freedom
should find its specific individual expression appears to have been
done away with along with the "Law."

This tradition seems to have made its first appearance in the enthusiasm
for freedom felt by the Corinthian church, which Paul had to rebut. For the
issue in the history of doctrine see the informative article by G. Kawerau,
"Antinomistische Streitigkeiten," RE, 3d ed., 1896, vol. I, 585ff. The struggle
which Luther waged against the "Antinomians" belongs to type four, discussed below.

2. The reproach of quietism has historically been brought against
the Lutheran tradition. This theme involves an interpretation of
justification by God, as a result of which the believers content themselves with the benefits of the life given to each of them and leave the
world outside to others. Thus it is easy to speak here of an "individualistic salvation," because the fulfillment of the individual's own
interest in salvation is such a person's only concern, and those concerns that should be served by freedom are perceived as irrelevant to
a life of faith.

Quietism was given prominence by E. Troeltsch in his *Die Soziallehren der
christlichen Kirchen und Gruppen, Gesammelte Werke*, vol. 1, esp. pp.
512ff. [*Social Teaching of the Christian Churches*, 1931]. Another interpretation was offered by W. Elert from a wide historical perspective in his *Mor-
phologie des Luthertums* (1931; 3d. ed. 1965).

3. Another result of the theoretical disturbance that can be produced by the doctrine of justification is the position that the outside world operates under its own laws. Faith and trust, and the life implicit in them would then be valid only for the relationship of humans to God, for the dimension of a *personal* and direct relation. The material and social aspects of life, on the other hand, operate according to laws that serve the goals of this world only and therefore are not touched by the attitude of faith. The ethic of faith deals only with conviction.

This theme was also discussed by Troeltsch in his presentation of Lutheran social ethics. See his *Soziallehren,* op. cit., p. 529 [*Social Teachings*]. H. Thielicke dealt with the problem in his *Theologische Ethik,* vol. 1, 1951. W. Huber analyzed the problem in terms of history of doctrine in "Eigengesetzlichkeit und Lehre von den Zwei Reichen," in N. Hasselmann, ed., *Gottes Wirken in seiner Welt. Zur Diskussion der Zwei-Reiche-Lehre,* vol. 2, 1980.

This opened the way for the tendency to hand the empirical world of affairs over to a practical atheism. In the present century this tendency has been countered by the revival of the doctrine of the two realms in which God rules. It seeks to express the insight that God does not rule the world only through the faith and activity of Christians, but also rules even where unbelieving and sinful humans do not seek to structure their lives in fellowship with God. The distinction between God's "spiritual" and "secular" ways of ruling the world has the result of speaking of God's presence and activity in the world independently of the subjective will of human beings. To be sure, the theological controversy about the exact nature of this distinction between the two ways in which God rules is at its core a debate about the way human beings function as Christians. In terms of knowledge the distinction between God's two ways of ruling is based on the doctrine of justification. Its content however relates the distinction directly to the relative (because indirectly perceived) independence of the presence of God in the world, in contrast to the always limited presence of the Christian.

The extensive discussion prior to 1966 is documented in the collection edited by H. H. Schrey, *Reich Gottes und Welt,* 1969. See also the introduction by G. Sauter in the volume of collected essays, *Zur Zwei-Reiche-Lehre* (*Theol. Bücherei* 49), 1973, pp. viiff.

4. Finally, a typology of erroneous solutions must also include the

negative dogmatism of a theory of justification that concerns itself with interpreting all human activity in terms of its reference to the individual self and of dealing exclusively with the theme of human sinfulness in all acts. In this way the doctrine of justification becomes a negative theory of achievement. This position does not go beyond describing human activity in its inevitable failure, its brokenness, and its shipwreck, and therefore fails to transform the dimension of action into a demonstration of the human need of justification.

This misunderstanding first arose out of problems in interpreting the doctrine of justification, which were already an issue in the sixteenth century in the writings of Agricola. (See the study made by W. Joest in his *Gesetz und Freiheit*, 1956.) Dietrich Bonhoeffer, in a frequently cited critique, attacked this widely popular misunderstanding. He urged that the gospel should be preached, not in a situation of "weakness" but in a situation of human "strength" (*Widerstand und Ergebung*, 6th ed., 1955, p. 182).

In coming to terms with these threats to the doctrine of justification it is necessary to set forth the ethical significance of the doctrine. For without the express explication of its ethical significance, justification tends to be turned into its opposite. I agree with Paul Althaus, who says "Luther's statement about faith first finds its full expression in ethics" (*Die Ethik Luthers*, 1965, p. 7).

It is probably a part of the reality of the conflict as it is defined by the doctrine of justification, that faith can be expressed as an intensified religious egoism. This would take the form of a theoretically successful realization of faith, successful because it is independent of one's own life and the conditions under which that life is lived. Thus it is possible that the striving for self-realization could succeed precisely at the heart of one's concern to live by faith.

Ethical theology, however, as a result of the doctrine of justification, must speak of a reformulation of the purpose of ethics. We can speak of such a reformulation if it is not the subject of the action that gives information about the action's purpose, but the world in which we live a life for others. For this reformulation the christological mediation of love is determinative. It means that the freedom which results from justification is not fulfilled in the good that accrues to the Christian who takes the actions. Individual Christians remain merely human beings, who in their empirical, social, and historical reality, in the place where they each lead their specific life, should be instruments for expressing the loving will of God. The Christian's righteousness and freedom are and continue to be a "iustitia aliena," a "foreign justice," dependent on its being mediated by Christ. The Christian is free in order to enter into the service of the community which God establishes with humanity.

3) Love as Life in Freedom

The redefinition of the purpose of ethics can best be made clear by reference to the classical text for reflection on love for one's neighbor, the parable of the Good Samaritan (Luke 10:19–33).

The question Jesus asks the disciples at the conclusion of the synoptic account is, "Which of these three, do you think, proved neighbor to the man who fell among the robbers?" And the answer is, "The one who showed mercy on him." The feature that defines love for one's neighbor is not to be found in the one who loves, his feelings, his attitude, his readiness to act. The distinctive feature is to be thought of as being in the one to whom we are or ought to be a neighbor. Love means providing for others a world in which to live, space for living, it means being the setting that others need in order to lead a good life. It is not in Christian intentions that we are aware of love, but in the "body," in "works," that is, in one's own empirical course of life. This is how the connection between human creatureliness and the love commandment is given concise expression.

In this sense we are justified in regarding the Christian concept of love as a modified utilitarianism. An ethic that follows the basic meaning of the love commandment is an ethic of results. It asks what consequences one's own actions and manner of life have for others, and on that basis lets itself be confirmed or corrected. It is not primarily ethics of convictions but ethics of responsibility. Its theme is not one's own perfection, one's own goodness, but the good in the transpersonal social context of what is useful, under the empirical conditions of real human existence, in terms of its limitations and tasks. This is what constitutes the realism of ethics.

But this has succeeded only in identifying the material framework of the ethical relevance of the love commandment. What does this mean for the agent of these actions? Christian ethics is not subject to an absolute command, and the quality of the Christian life cannot be measured by ethical rigorism. The commitment to freedom protects us from such human arrogance as finds expression in an exaggerated claim to the validity of Christian behavior. Christianity is not the solution to the world's problems, but it does increase our sensitivity to them.

The perception of the love commandment always brings into question a Christian's relationship to himself or herself; it brings into question one's willingness to sacrifice self, which we must always affirm in opposition to our tendency toward self-realization. Thus ethical experience is also an appeal to the renewal of faith and of trust in the reality of freedom, which must be taken into account by anyone who wants or should want to act in the spirit of love. This connection between the "external" utility of our actions and the "internal" commitment to the ethical meaning of freedom is what must be transmitted in ethical theology.

4) Renewing the Meaning of Creation

Is it possible to command love? This question implies that love has to do with directness and spontaneity, that it must be practiced of itself and cannot take the form of an alien command, "Love!" Does this mean that love is irrational? Is it not open to any rational insight? Does the love commandment therefore confront us with the demand to wait until love arises of itself, so that when this does not happen we can still not say that it is "commanded"?

It is significant that traditionally it has always been the case that love is seen where people do the required good of their own free will, without being compelled to do so. To this extent the rationality of the love commandment consists in its defining the fulfillment of the command "from within." In an emphatic sense Christians do not need any external commands because they perform for their own reasons, because of love, that which otherwise laws and commands compel and force people to do. But even so it is appropriate to speak of a love commandment, because in it the intention of all commandments whatsoever is given expression.

It is not the case that the love commandment forms the basis of any specific group of norms in contrast to other norms. Love as living for others or as constituting a world for others is the inner purpose of all actions. Thus, in terms of the theological premises developed here, a life in love can be understood as the realization of that which ethical theory has traditionally sought to express by the term "highest good."

Recently theology has seen love as the form of life in community with God, especially as a harbinger of the kingdom of God, and has brought it into connection with the concepts of eschatology.

W. Pannenberg proposed this explicitly in his book *Theologie und Reich Gottes*, 1971, especially in the section "Das Problem einer Begründung der Ethik und die Gottesherrschaft," pp. 63–78.

All this serves to point up by contrast the considerate, productive nature of activity that results from love, which enables us to go beyond convenient considerations of value and usefulness. Our attention will focus on the insight that the forming of the world in which we live always implies its renewal, the concrete anticipation of that which does not yet exist empirically, but which can be anticipated as the ultimate community of God and human beings in activity based on love, in the overcoming of alienation and conflict. Love can then be seen as active attentiveness to the renewal of the meaning the world was given at creation, which awakens an ethically responsible imagination and creativity in the service of the good.

3. The Third Basic Element: Reflection on Life

As the theory of how to live one's life, ethics is an academic discipline and therefore a purely theoretical undertaking. The theory however, cannot be regarded as superior to life but must be seen in proper perspective. Thus to specify reflection on life as the third basic element in the reality of the ethical life is to call our attention to the fact that ethical reflection is not merely the privilege of the theoretical ethicist but also has a role to play in the actual living of life. The possibility of constructing a specifically ethical theory of how to live is therefore rooted in the public and open reality of life as it is dealt with in reflective thought. Theory building cannot escape this state of affairs, because in its limited, academic manner it too involves reflection on life. This will be explored concisely in the following paragraphs.

a. The Fullness of Life

Any discussion of the reflection that is immanent in the reality of life must take into account the fullness of life. We become aware that many more factors are involved than can be exhausted in a single lifetime. This superfluity of reality can be experienced as a challenge, but as an indistinct challenge of possibilities, in the face of which humans become aware of their finitude. Finitude is an expression of our relationship to the fullness of life which can never be exhausted in those experiences which we actually realize in life or in the specific forms that life takes. This is not the same as speaking of the fullness and power of the human subject, of the subject's productivity.

The desired productivity, which makes the subject aware of finitude, grows out of participation in the varied possibilities that confront us.

This is the context in which we encounter the specifically modern experience of the historical nature of human life. It is only in part identical with those interpretations of human conduct that are expressed in the much lamented relativism of norms and relationships. The experience of historicity is an experience of the fullness of life, because our historical consciousness keeps ever before us the immense variety of human styles and modes of action. At the specific time in which we live we can feel the challenge of alternatives from another time as still being present reality, as presenting the possibility of leading our lives in a different manner. At no time can it be absolutely determined what is truly appropriate to that specific time. Our historical consciousness keeps alternatives alive, and they remain alternatives even though they can no longer be experienced or cannot be experienced concretely again.

The structure of such reflection on life becomes ethically relevant because it allows us to discover possibilities that constitute the boundaries of humanity in its concrete reality. These boundaries make us aware of the differences between an individual life and life in general, and they demand that we take a stand. To state it formally, reflection is distancing ourselves from specific factors in which the givenness of life becomes concrete. But this distancing is and remains a reflective action. It is not really distancing ourselves or really changing our position. But it makes us aware as humans of our role as subjects in our world, a world which is not simply at our disposal and which does not make it possible for us to have absolute control over our life. Instead, it enables us to participate in the fullness of life.

Compare the discussion of ethical theory as the establishing of limits on our subjectivity in T. Rendtorff, "Religion als Thema wissenschaftlicher Theoriebildung oder das Subject interdisziplinärer Orientierung," in R. Schwarz, ed., *Wissenschaft als interdisziplinäres Problem. Internationales Jahrbuch für interdisziplinäre Forschung,* 1974, pp. 375ff.

In this sense, reflection on life sets the theme for a relationship to reality, a relationship that transcends present reality even in the midst of that reality, and by so doing lays a claim on humanity beyond what is present. Even if it is true that such reflective thought deals exclusively with its human subject, it would still be saying too little if we were to define it exclusively in anthropocentric terms. The fullness of life as a reality that calls for reflection can be regarded as the religious dimension of life, because in it we can achieve a knowledge of a relationship of all reality to God as the subject of all reality. But even religion, where it becomes specific, that is to say, historical, is unable to exhaust that fullness. The fact that religion exists only in the plurality of the religions, that religious knowledge can only take shape as a relationship to something that lies beyond itself, shows that religion is also the expression and the channel of a life in relation to the fullness of life. In all the aspects mentioned here it can be seen that ethical reflection is a necessary way for humans to take a stand in relation to the fullness of life.

b. The Necessity of an Orientation for Life

On the basis of the fullness of life, it is necessary to speak of the need for orientation. The cases where it is obvious how we should live, where we know without asking what we should do and how we should live, do not constitute the whole of life. When we look at life as a whole, the need for orientation is dominant at the beginning and at the end of life. It applies equally to the presuppositions and the goals of our actions and makes the experienced person and the inexperienced equal. The need for orientation is inherent in human speech. Speaking is a permanent process of seeking to orient ourselves, to achieve certainty and understanding. Analyses in theoretical linguistics show that we can regard human speech as an indication that living involves reflection.

For the relationship of language and ethics, see I. Dalferth and E. Jüngel, "Sprache als Träger von Sittlichkeit," in *Handbuch der christlichen Ethik*, vol. 2, pp. 454–73.

Language places the individual life in the wider context of the whole of life. It can do so only because it constitutes an independent context in its logic and its symbols. Ethical reflection always involves speaking about the relationship of things to each other; it is as much involved in reality as ordinary conversation is, but in this relationship it requires a certain distancing of itself in language.

The significance of this for ethics is that human speech calls attention to the human capability of error in the conduct of life. Distancing oneself by the use of language is basically the possibility of becoming aware of an unsuccessful orientation, aware of failure in dealing with the realities of one's own life. The ethical measure of an error is not expressed in a simple "false" or "true," but rather on a continuum of successful or unsuccessful dealings with the tasks of life, of whether we are able to go forward or not. Language provides productive relationships by showing us a way to find the orientation we need. By bringing to pass something that was not yet reality, speech becomes a part of reflection on life. It enables us to deal with errors and mistakes, and thus brings into play something that goes beyond reality.

But it can also fall into error, because it is ambiguous. This ambiguity remains even in cases where we can assert that we have experienced clarity. This is shown by the history of those religious and secular doctrines of revelation that are based on language and rely on the spoken word. Thus our use of speech does not do away with the necessity of leading our own lives, any more than does scientific knowledge of the world in which we live.

c. *Transcendence Through Communication*

The reality of a life is not exhausted in the meaning derived from its purposes and goals. Ethical reflection is a dimension of our social nature, an anticipation of community, which is achieved through the development of the capacity to communicate. Thus transcendence based on communication is also relevant. Not only what we express through speech and gestures but also what we produce and what we do has an effect on the way we lead our lives, and they must be taken into account in the context of interpersonal communication. It is not those who can do whatever they want who are free, but those who can be called to accountability for the way they lead their lives. But then if freedom implies a dependence on communication, it also transcends the possibilities that individuals have at their disposal.

Ethical reflection which takes place in an awareness that our lives are lived in a transcendence derived from communication constitutes the public nature of one's personal life. Our circumstances are the forum in which those around us share with us in deciding how our lives are lived. By extending the immediate relevance of our interests in life to include the society of all who are alive, we take a step toward a perception of our own lives as they are seen by those around us from their own point of view. To see oneself with the eyes of others can be regarded as the elementary presence of transcendence in the way we lead our own lives. The theological dimension of this transcendence through communication is expanded when we speak of living "in the presence of God." In this public communication the course of life and the way we change that course become themes for consideration. The continuity of life becomes significant for our whole outlook, which includes more than the specific time and place at which we act. Such

an outlook is a basic development growing out of the theory. This theoretical outlook in one's own life is expressed by the ethical term
"responsibility." Responsibility presupposes the capability of correct-
ing oneself in the forum of public communication, of learning that
we have our own identity only as an unfolding public identity.

Finally, transcendence through communication can culminate in
the challenge to "become all things to all men" (1 Cor. 9:22), as the
apostle Paul endeavored to do in his missionary task. That is a concept by which a person lives all of life in the service of communicating the whole of life. Taking up this role involves setting goals that
transcend one's own self-realization, and that culminate in communication with others. In all of this, however, our lives are still in need
of proper orientation. Orientation to different goals leads to different
types of reflection. This is the basis of the competition between
specific formulations of ethical reflection, which in itself is a communication event. But these differences can no longer be ironed out by
reference to indirect evidence derived from ethical data. They force
us, as a result of the theoretical implications of ethical reflection, to
ask what is the goal that is determinative for our life in community.

d. Faith as the Anticipation of Success

Ethical reflection grows out of the experience that each person must
lead his or her own life, in full awareness of dependence on society
and of the claims of society. This experience becomes reflective when
the individual recognizes how limited one's power over circumstances
is. When reflection on life is intensified we can speak of faith. Faith
is the anticipation of success in life under three conditions: empirically experienced finitude, the possibility that our attempts to give
direction to our lives will fail, and transcendence through communication. Faith as the anticipation of success provides good grounds in
each person's life for committing oneself, in the knowledge that one's
powers are limited, without becoming irritated that the completion
of our ethical tasks cannot be taken for granted.

This line of argument was developed by F. Kambartel in his article "Theo-
Logisches. Definitorische Vorschläge zu einigen Grundtermini im Zusammenhang christlicher Rede von Gott." ZEE 15 (1971): 32–35.

This is where the connection of ethics with faith, which is so
characteristic of Christianity, begins. Faith as the belief, in the face
of all the facts, that one will succeed in life, takes its orientation from

that type of anticipation which is represented by Jesus Christ and expressed theoretically by the doctrine of justification.

W. Härle called this the "greatest achievement" of the doctrine of justification: "Even where people contradict their humanity through their deeds, their deeds still do not destroy their humanity or even set it aside." "Humanität. Überlegungen zum Verhältnis von Anthropologie und Ethik," in H. Fischer, ed., *Anthropologie als Thema der Theologie*, 1978, p. 127. To be sure, it is the positive application of this state of affairs that gives expression to what the doctrine of justification symbolizes. Although the dogmatic formulation of this anticipation does not correspond to the logic of this expression, ethical theology sees in it the significance of faith for the conduct of one's life. The difference between life that is given and life that is surrendered is perceived through reflection, and the acceptance of the difference can then be seen as something good.

Faith is the form of ethical reflection that bridges the gap between our limited human ability and success in life, because it is God who takes over the responsibility for ultimate success. In this way those who believe are enabled, within their own limits, to affirm that they are to work for success in life in their own individual way. On the other hand, we must reject any definition of the relationship between ethics and faith in which human ethics is regarded as a system that is doomed to impotence, while faith shares God's power and therefore can be termed, in and of itself, an ethic of success. The confusion that this produces can be seen when "faith" is regarded as expressing an ethic that is in competition with humanistic ethics. The claim that faith has moved beyond the difference between the conduct of the individual human life on the one hand and a successful life on the other would rob faith of the liberating function that it can play in clarifying the difference between the two. Such an understanding of faith would tend to become mere ideology, because the empirical nature of the ethical reality of life would be eliminated from the concept of faith.

e. The Future of the Good

When we regard ethics as dealing with the challenge to place our lives in the service of the good, we take it for granted that the good has not yet fully become reality. This "not yet" expresses the time element in the ethical reality of life as an orientation to the future. This orientation is present wherever the question is raised of how to solve the ethical task, and the path is specified on which the good is to become reality.

The future orientation of life can be reflected in the demand that people transform their own lives into good lives. Changing the way we live brings the future into the time in which we are living in the sense of a "new" or "renewed" life. The transformation of one's own style of life brings one nearer to the "not yet" of the good. However it is not only the individual human being but the world of humanity that is not yet perfected. The future is a dimension of life because it makes reflective thought about the reality of life into a major theme. This "not yet" includes the experiences that have been described above as the oppressiveness of the fullness of life, as the need for an orientation of life, and as transcendence through communication, as well as the anticipation of success through faith and trust.

Concrete concepts of the future and expectations of what it will bring are first of all the extrapolation of problems and conflicts in the way we are living, extrapolations that seek solutions. We can see them as problems and conflicts only because the future good has ontological precedence over the present life.

With the term "ontological precedence of the good," W. Pannenberg attempted to specify the ethical relevance of eschatology and above all the symbol of "kingdom of God" (*Theologie und Reich Gottes*, 1971, p. 69). The symbol "kingdom of God" means that human reality is not exhausted in what is present, but that humanity is called to fellowship with God. In reference to human working and striving, the future-related nature of life expresses the theme of the permanent difference between God and humankind. But it also challenges us, by reflecting on life, to discover and acknowledge the appropriate way in which humans can participate in fellowship with God and unite their own activity with the "dynamic of God's affirmation of the world" (Pannenberg, op. cit., p. 71).

The future does not do away with ethics but rather gives it new meaning in its specific religious function. To be sure, the religious expectation of the future may tend to see the future as the negation of the present world, the world that is "perishing." But that would be a future in which humans would no longer have any meaningful tasks to perform. Thus even faith in the future stands in need of a new theoretical formulation. The ethical relevance of the future becomes the question of the relevance of ethics for the expectation of the future. Such expectation that has been the object of ethical reflection resists any negation of the given world for the sake of the future good, and instead acknowledges the future as an element in the life that has been given to us as our responsibility. In this sense we are directed once again to the beginning of the discussion which introduced the ethical task.

PART THREE

THE METHODOLOGY OF ETHICS

1. The Three Methodological Aspects of the Ethical Question

a. On the Methodology of Ethics

If we define ethics as the theory of how we are to live, we are led to analyze the ethical question, and to describe and emphasize its basic elements. Now that these basic elements involved in living an ethical life have been described, we must look at the various elements of the ethical question in a methodical fashion so that they can be carefully considered. This will strengthen the role of ethics in orienting the discussion of how human life is to be lived. An ethical methodology of this sort is highly desirable, because the complexity of ethical experience demands a high degree of clarity, and clarity must extend to all the varied aspects that constitute ethical problems.

This approach breaks new ground in that as a rule the theological literature on ethics moves from the basic elements to a direct consideration of specific themes of the so-called practical ethical problems. This customary procedure makes it difficult to see the connection between the details of the basic discussion and the concrete issues in ethics. To avoid the impression of arbitrariness, it is necessary to return to the basic question when each specific ethical theme is discussed.

The approach adopted here makes it possible to enter into discussion with the various academic approaches that are significant for ethics today. Thus our methodology can take into account the insight that a theory of ethics grows out of the debate with the experience of reality. We must be on our guard against any attempt to develop an ethic from a single normative theological approach.

E. Troeltsch was quite right in stating "that morality is by its very nature not a unity, but is highly complex, that humans grow up with a variety of ethical goals, the unification of which constitutes the problem, not the starting point" (*Grundprobleme der Ethik, Gesammelte Werke*, vol. 2, 1962, p. 657). This pluralism must be taken into account in any detailed analysis.

A. Gehlen advanced the anthropological thesis that "being human involves

85

a pluralism of moral issues," by which he was saying that an "ethos all of one piece" is always the result of a specific historical and sociological process, in which a scientific approach must always discern a pluralism of starting points (*Moral und Hypermoral. Eine pluralistische Ethik*, 1968, p. 38). The theoretical undertaking which this requires must make explicit the various elements which play a role in the formation of an ethic, and then discuss them in their highly differentiated relationship to each other.

In the light of the various scientific aspects which must be taken into account here, this present attempt can make no claim to completeness. For example, the issues raised by an anthropology oriented to biology and the natural sciences will play a lesser role than those raised by sociology or the various positions of practical philosophy. The significant thing is that the debate with the variety of ethical data must be accorded its proper place in the construction of an ethic.

By the methodology of ethics we are able to understand the precise following of a process in which the basic structure of ethics as set forth above is explored and analyzed in its details. Such a methodology is consistent with the belief that ethics can not only be developed in general principles, but can involve also the individualized and concrete discussion of its principles, and becomes changed in the process. This involves the function of ethics that takes reality into account.

b. The Basic Starting Point:
What Should We Do?

As our starting point I have chosen the simple question, What should we do? It involves the element of reflection on ethical questions, which we have been discussing, but now in a more specialized form. The question, What should we do? contains the structure of the answer. It is a reaction to the challenge of leading one's own life. It arises in the context of our life when in a specific case or a general manner people feel questioned about their own place in the world and before God.

In the most elementary form we encounter the question as that which the "people," the "tax collectors" or the "soldiers" ask of John the Baptist (Luke 2:10, 12, 14) or which the "Israelites" ask Peter (Acts 2:37, 38).

It is methodologically permissible to take up the question of a specific context in order to let it play a role in ethical theory as a question involving ethical reflection. It can be understood as a reaction to the fact that people as ethical subjects/agents are challenged to do what is good. The reflective structure of the question establishes a difference between action in general and the "what" of a specific activity. It is elementary in nature since reflection on it shows that the one asking the question is, as one about to act, not committed to taking a specific action, but must express himself or herself in the action, must determine to take the action. It requires an answer, and to be answered it must move beyond the immediate context. The chain of events in an active life is broken. The ethical question alters the way in which a person lives. Thus the extent and the direction of the change are determined by the nature of the answer.

In the context of the questions taken above as examples, this happens through specific, unusual demands made by Jesus or through a thorough-going call to repentence by Peter. It is not a matter of mere reflection. The question, What should we do? seeks for information about the meaning of a specific situation for one's own actions. If we broaden the scope of the question, we are asking, What is really significant for human beings? What is the reality in which they really live? The purpose of the question is to bring to our consciousness our place in reality and our active participation in it. It thus involves nor only specific suggestions for action and direct instruction. It is also concerned with one's position and attitude toward life, toward one's self, and toward others. It is designed to this extent to help us rediscover the relationship that ethical questions have to reality as discussed above in Part II. Ethics involves more than questions for information. It involves what is ethically relevant, that is, that which concerns our relationship to reality as it bears on the way in which we live our lives.

Kant's phrasing of the question "What should I do?" as the "practical" or "moral" question pointed in this direction (*Kritik der reinen Vernunft (Critique of Pure Reason)*, PhB 37a, ed. R. Schmidt, 1956, p. 728). W. Trillhaas had commented that this question is "too narrow" because it does not cover the "breadth of human behavior" as individuals as well as in society (*Ethik*, 1959, p. 1). This objection is relevant if the question obscured the fact that it is meaningful only in a larger context of reality. Human actions are always related to the world, history, and community, and without these relationships they cannot be explained and understood. E. Jüngel also rejected this question of Kant's, saying that "it is oriented only to the individual," and "makes it necessary that we answer the question with an abstract recurring to the principle of a law-giving that is valid for the sum total of all historically possible individuals." He suggested instead that we should ask a question that provides a concrete unity of all humans in a community, "What is to be done?" ("Erwägungen zur Grundlegung evangelischer Ethik im Anschlus an die Theologie des Paulus," in *Unterwegs zur Sache*, 1972, p. 235.) In this critique, interest in the relationship of the ethical question to reality is dominant. But the impersonal form in which Jüngel casts the question does not give full expression to the need for reflection that is involved in the ethical question.

It goes without saying that such a question should not be overloaded with interpretations. It can serve its methodological function as the starting point for raising the issue of the reflective nature of ethics, if it is phrased so as to lead us into the various dimensions of the ethical question.

c. The Three Methodological Aspects of the Question, What Should We Do?

The initial question, What should we do? proves on examination to be no simple question. It contains three dimensions which can now serve as the three basic methodological aspects of ethics. They can be formulated as three typical answers that can be proposed to the initial question.

1) The Answer of Tradition: Rules Ethics

The question, What should we do? can first of all be answered by reference to the commandments. For example, Obey God's commands. The counter question, What are God's commands? can be answered by pointing to the Decalogue as the list of the most basic commands. But the possible answers are not exhausted in this reference. The answer could also go, Do what your parents and teachers have told you to do. Do what morality and law require. Obey the constitution of the country in which you live. The empirical completeness of the possible answers or a specific list of such answers is not what is at stake, but rather the structure of the answer.

We can imagine an answer or a group of answers which assert that the question, "What should we do?" has already been answered, and tell how it has been answered. When the ethical question is raised in a real case or because of a specific stimulus, it can be dealt with by pointing to answers that have already been given. These answers we may term the answer of the ethical tradition.

Following the traditional terminology of ethics and morality we can also speak of a "duty ethic."

In any case, ethics is required to follow a path in which these possible answers are examined and their meaning set forth in detail. All expressions that refer to commandments, which speak of ordinances, which have the nature of a command, or which cite norms or standards which are already in force belong to the answer of the ethical tradition. This first of the possible answers can be called a "Rules ethic."

Theological ethics are usually presented as rules ethics. P. Althaus defines the task of ethics as that of presenting the teaching of what Christian thought "knows about obedience to God's commands," and begins with a consideration of the commandments (*Grundriss der Ethik*, 2d ed., 1959, pp. 11, 17ff.). K. Barth subsumes ethics under the theme, "The reality of the divine commands" as "the commands that are given us concerning what is good" (*Ethik* I, 1928, 1973, p. 103). E. Brunner gave his "Draft of a Protestant Theological Ethic" the title, *Das Gebot und die Ordnungen* (1932; 4th ed., 1939; ET: *The Divine Imperative*, 1937). H. G. Fritzsche wrote an ethics which explicitly followed the schema of the Ten Commandments, *Evangelische Ethik. Die Gebote Gottes als Grundprinzipien christlichen Handelns*, 3d ed., 1966. G. Ebeling wrote an interpretation of the Ten Commandments in the form of sermons (*Die zehn Gebote*, 1973). Treatments of the Decalogue itself include Bo Reicke, *Die zehn Worte in Geschichte und Gegenwart*, 1973, and Hendrik van Oyen, *Ethik des Alten Testamentes*, 1967, pp. 102–32.

What are the distinguishing structural features of this answer to our question? The answer of the ethical tradition or of rules ethics points the questioner to an already existing authority. This means first of all that they point the questioner to answers that have earlier been given by other persons, in contrast to one's own commandment, a maxim of action that is a personal choice. This must be accepted as a meaningful answer which is actually given in many cases. This answer places the individual's life in the context of a larger community and points to orientations that are valid beyond the needs of any individual. Thus there are no reasonable grounds for rejecting this answer.

But it must be immediately added that this answer does not exhaust the ethical question. It can be an adequate answer in specific cases, but it cannot be a complete answer. Counter questions can be raised, for example, Who says what the valid tradition is and what is commanded in that tradition? The counter question can bring ethical reflection into play in such a manner that we are reminded that the tradition has a starting point and a history. It can advance the argument that perhaps different or new answers are possible. But it is possible to conceive of a counter question which would ask, Why should I follow the tradition or the commandments? This makes us aware that an ethical tradition does not simply stand on unquestioned authority, but has gained its position out of the experiences of life through which it has been authenticated. Without this experiential knowledge of its authentication it is impossible to hand down the tradition. Thus an ethical tradition always implies a specific world. And every new ethical question raises the problem whether and how the existing world can become, and can remain, our own world. However the counter questions are phrased in detail, the original question must be expressed in such a way that it can be the questioners' own, or that they can adopt for themselves the answer that the tradition offers.

2) The Answer of the Conduct of One's Own Life: Responsibility Ethics

The question, What should we do? can be answered in a second manner by reference to one's personal responsibility.

You yourself must know what you should do! Only be sure that you do what is good and right! Don't be misled by prejudices, by hasty feelings or false caution. You must assume the responsibility for whatever you do. Answers from this second point of view have as their goal individuals who can themselves become ethical agents. They are to assume a "moral standpoint" and not simply let the answer be given them from outside. They themselves must search for the answer. The possibility of answering in this manner opens our eyes to the present reality of ethical decision making. It confronts the questioners themselves, their position, their readiness to participate in exploring the ethical question. In this sense the answer can be provided, for example, by pointing to the command to love, "You shall love the Lord your God . . . You shall love your neighbor as yourself" (Matt. 22:37, 38). The issue is not the adequacy of the various ways in which this answer is interpreted; the issue is the structure of the answer.

We can also imagine an answer or group of answers that express the way in which the question, What should we do? bears on our responsibility and our decision making. In a current issue or a specific situation, the ethical question becomes the question of how we live our own lives. Therefore we sum up the nature of this answer as the answer of the conduct of one's own life. If we employ the traditional terminology of ethics and morality, we might speak here of an ethic of character.

Ethics must therefore open up a way for this answer to be given. This possibility is present wherever those who question are aware that the answer, however it might be phrased, is something that they must deal with. It assumes the form of an ethical decision, in the sense that those who question must form their own judgment and express themselves in their actions. It would be eccentric, however, to picture the situation where such a decision is required as that of an isolated individual all alone in a private world. Situations where reality is experienced are determinative for our decisions, but these are situations that either have their own individual character and thus cannot simply be judged by a general rule, or they are entirely new and therefore demand a new solution. In our present situation of rapid change this is often the case. However this state of affairs may be described in detail, those who act must express themselves in their actions. This second possible answer can therefore be termed responsibility ethics.

The ethical task can be understood as responsibility ethics when theology is done in continuity with the historical-critical study of Scripture, that is to say, in the framework of an understanding of reality that seeks to do justice to the subjectivity of all reality. In this way all references made by ethics to reality fall under the comprehensive point of view of responsibility. This is the case with Friedrich Gogarten (*Der Mensch zwischen Gott und Welt*, 1952; *Verhängnis und Hoffnung der Neuzeit*, 1953) or with Rudolf Bultmann (for example in "Neues Testament und Mythologie," 1942, in *Kerygma und Mythos* I, 1948, esp. pp. 38ff.). For a discussion of Bultmann's thought see H.-E. Tödt, *Die Ethik R. Bultmanns*, 1978. So-called situation ethics also belongs here, as it was expressly advocated by J. Fletcher, *Situation Ethics. The New Morality*, 1966.

Are these two answers mutually exclusive? Are they alternative answers? Before the ethical theorists give in to the inclination to construct alternatives they must first consider the arguments against doing so. The difference between the alternatives, as well as their respective contexts must be counted part of the complexity of the ethical reality of life, which forbids us to work with a simple either-or model. There is no contradiction between the two possible answers that have been discussed here. They are not mutually exclusive. The difference between them is primarily that they differ in specifying the subject that gives the answer. The first answer points to a subject different from the one who is posing the question. The subject of the command is God, or one's parents, tradition, and so forth, that is to say, in each case someone or something other than the one questioning. The second answer, on the contrary, appeals directly to the one questioning as being the ethical subject. It expects that the questioner will respond in the same manner as the subject in the case of the first answer.

The limitations of both possible answers may be described by saying that even rules ethics demands that the one asking the question become involved. Commandments too must always be expressed in individual terms and applied to current situations.

This found a very direct expression in the formation of casuistry, which sought to make individualized interpretations of general rules for decisions in individual lives. Casuistry has its "Sitz-im-Leben" in the practice of confession and penance. It has the twofold goal of integrating individuals into the general ethical tradition and at the same time applying general rules to individual human lives. A casuistry that was consistently carried out would turn itself into an autonomous responsibility ethics, if it really took seriously the fact that each individual life constitutes a new example of life in general.

But even if we begin with the second answer we encounter limitations. Responsibility ethics is not satisfied with the historically-given ethical judgment of tradition. For what counts as a commandment in a historical sense must be valid in an unconditioned sense and therefore in the present time must have its autonomous basis. This does not mean that ethical responsibility is without context and can act in accord with whatever point of view it pleases. It also in every instance constitutes the beginning of an individual tradition. The connections that are identified here do not, however, do away with the differences between the two answers. They must be respected and followed out further, because only so can the complexity of the ethical question be brought to light. But the reflections that have been presented here show that even taking the two answers together does not exhaust the possibilities, but that they belong to the context of the same ethical discourse which holds for all specific ethics.

3) *The Task of the Theoretical Justification of Ethics: Metaethics*

The question, What should we do? can in the third place be answered by the challenge to become involved in the evaluation of ethical judgments. For example, how can we know whether tradition and its rules are justified? On what basis do we appeal to our own responsibility? What means are at our disposal for dealing with the rightness of the duties laid upon us?

Answers from this third point of view have moral discourse itself as their theme. They involve us in that careful scrutiny which is demanded by every serious ethical question. Ethical discourse involves reflecting collectively on what we really consider the good to be and on what reasons we have for doing so. As a rule it is bound up with ethical activity. The ethical task does not consist in confronting individual actions or decisions, or in series of actions or decision processes alone. Ethical reflection can itself become a theme for reflection. The examination of ethical judgments and rules is a way of choosing and setting priorities.

We saw earlier that this testing plays a significant role in New Testament ethics (see above, p. 20). This is vital for Christianity and the ethical culture which it has shaped. For Christianity does not lend itself to being forced into a narrowly defined ethical program of rules and norms, nor does it proclaim an absolute freedom. Rather, by accepting and rejecting elements of contemporary morality it has sought to impart meaning and direction to its own ethic. This is not the place to enter into a full presentation of the historical and systematic elements of this approach. Our concern is to call attention to the independence of this dimension of ethical reflection. Thus we can imagine an answer, or a group of answers to the question, What should we do? that would constitute a part of a permanent ethical discourse. The ethical question itself becomes a task that requires independent reflection and testing. The answer that can be given here leads us thus into the task of the theoretical justification of ethics.

If we employ the traditional concepts of moral discourse and ethics this is the place for dealing with the doctrine of the good, or the doctrine of the highest good. It is not possible to pursue further in any meaningful way the question of a theoretical justification of ethics without taking into account the issue of the content of a "highest good" or its equivalent. Ethics must therefore be approached as a path on which this task receives proper attention.

The task of a theoretical justification and investigation of ethics plays today, especially in the discussion in Anglo-Saxon lands, a highly significant role. As far as I can see, contemporary discussions of metaethics are not concerned with such questions of content as are involved in the doctrine of the "highest good." A good discussion of the history of metaethics in this century is found in A. Pieper, "Analytische Ethik. Ein Überblick über die seit 1900 in England und Amerika erschienene Ethikliteratur," *Philosophisches Jahrbuch* 78, 1971, pp. 144ff. But in any case the task constituted by metaethics is not the special preserve of the Anglo-Saxon ethical tradition.

Above all this task deserves attention because it presents us with a situation in which the historical clarity and finality of ethical traditions have given way to a pluralism of ethical orientations, and in which the assurance of individual moral autonomy has yielded place to the experience of the social nature of all ethical decisions. The ethical task that has arisen here can thus be included under metaethics.

Metaethics in the Anglo-Saxon sense has until now found only hesitant acceptance in the discussion of Protestant ethics. An interesting example of a metaethical approach to theological ethics is found in A. Jeffner, "Die Rechtfertigung ethischer Urteile," ZEE 19 (1975): 234ff. In discussions in German similar methodological investigations have been carried out by G. Sauter, for example in the collection he edited, *Wissenschaftstheoretische Kritik der Theologie. Die Theologie und die neuere wissenschaftstheoretische Discussion*, 1973. H .-E. Tödt undertook to construct a theoretical guide to actions in "Versuch zu einer Theorie ethischer Urteilsfindung," ZEE 21 (1977): 81–93. For the subsequent discussion see O. Höffe, "Bermerkungen zu einer Theorie sittlicher Urteilsfinding," ZEE 22 (1978): 181–87, and Chr. Frey, "Humane Erfahrung und selbstkritische Vernunft," ZEE 22 (1978): 200–213.

The term metaethics clearly expresses the distinction between it and the first two dimensions of ethical answers. Metaethics presupposes ethics in the sense of a rules ethic or a responsibility ethic. It relates to them and cannot and does not want to replace them. Its intention is to be exclusively ethical theory. But it would be foolish not to regard it as a dimension of the ethical reality of life, because metaethics explicitly presents the theme of ethical discourse which is always present in ethics. Only when we remain aware of this connection and do not absolutize the theoretical task do we pursue a path on which the theoretical justification of ethics itself takes on ethical significance.

These three possible answers describe the content of ethical methodology. The answer of the ethical tradition, rules ethics; the answer of leading one's own life, responsibility ethics; and the answer of the justification of ethic, metaethics. These are the three basic methodological aspects which must now be investigated in detail.

2. The Methodological Structure of Ethics

a. The Structure of Ethics According to Ethical Tradition

What points of view are most significant for the structure of ethics when we approach the problem in terms of ethical tradition?

We now turn to the first group of answers which are concerned with the data relevant for ethics, data which every ethic must take into account, because they are the givens in every formation of an ethical judgment. These are structural elements which demand our attention if we are to form ethical judgments or construct an ethical way of life that corresponds to reality. The goal that is set for us here is to determine the significance which the perception of reality has for ethics.

Thus an investigation of the answer which the ethical tradition provides must specify in detail the factors that are the givens of life, the basic situation of ethics (see above, p. 33). We must develop lines of argument that are able to show that what in some sense ought to be, actually occurs, and thus actually is. This problem, so pressing for ethics, is expressed colloquially in the sceptical comment that an ethical demand is "merely" an ethical conviction, but has nothing to do with reality. It involves an ethical ideal that is out of touch with reality and therefore not practical. This apparent powerlessness of our ethical consciousness is something that we must take seriously. It cannot simply be refuted by counter assertions; we must accept it as a challenge to work out an ethic that explicitly considers the question of the relationship of ethics to reality. This question is accompanied by the insight that the answer of the ethical tradition in the sense in which it is spoken of here includes the claim that ethics gives expression to the obligatory character of the reality of human life and is therefore not a mere expression of intentions.

The starting point for the further questions involved here is the proposition that ethics always implies a world.

If we take this basic premise seriously, an important methodological decision has already been made. We must reject any approach that excludes from ethics everything that could be regarded as capable of being observed or determined empirically, so that nothing was left for ethics except intentions, sentiment, and rules. We must not hold that any reality perceived empirically is irrelevant for ethics, but on the contrary we must be entirely clear about its relevance. To be sure there are reasons today for ethics as an academic discipline to beware of too-close proximity to empirically oriented social sciences, first because there are so many details that it is impossible to master them, but also because of the methodological complications that appear in any scientifically oriented approach. But wariness may help us keep our eyes open. It can help us avoid taking everything as our theme simply because everything is relevant, but instead to work out in each specific case the appropriate ethical point of view according to which empirical reality is necessarily a concern of ethics. And at the same time it may free us from the compulsion to enter into immediate competition in ethical discussion with those who have expert knowledge. The basic premise that ethics always implies a world will now be explored in five areas, which in a general way correspond to the five points involved in the first of the basic elements of the reality of life dealt with above.

1) From Factual Knowledge to the Formation of a World View

"Frequently, when someone is unclear as to what he or someone else should do in an specific situation, what is needed is not ethical instruction, but simply a better knowledge of the facts or greater conceptual clarity" (W. Frankena, *Ethics*, 1963, p. 11). This statement of Frankena's is a good introduction to the starting point from which we can move to a perception of reality in its ethical significance. We can think of a person in a difficult situation who does not know what to do. He is then encouraged to describe his situation once again. It is a frequent experience that in describing and evaluating more carefully the actual situation, in identifying what the situation is, many aspects of the problem become clearer.

The search for ways of dealing with such questions is widespread. A. Jeffner and J. Hemberg have presented examples drawn from discussions in Scandinavia of how ethicists can develop moral discourse in cooperation with experts in various fields (A. Jeffner, "Die Rechtfertigung ethischer Urteile," ZEE 19 (1975): 234–48; J. Hemberg, "Ethik in Schweden. Die Diskussion der 70er Jahre," ZEE 21 (1977): 241–56). For the discussion in the Netherlands, see C. J. Dippel, R. Kwant, H. v. Riessen, J. Voogd, *Research en Ethiek*, 1962; P. J. Roscam Abbing, *Om den Mens. Ethiek en wetenshap en beroep*, 1968. For ethical study in North America, see G. Winter, *Elements for a Social Ethics*, 1966, and M. L. Stackhouse, "Gesellschaftstheorie und Sozialethik," in ZEE 22 (1978): 275–95. In discussions in the German language, the call for interdisciplinary efforts in ethics has elicited a variety of responses from theologians. One outcome of this movement is E. Herms's presentation of basic considerations in *Theologie als Erfahrungswissenschaft*, 1978.

In this present work the entire question has been accorded an appropriate place in developing the fundamentals of ethics. The concrete discussions in Part Four present more material.

At the opposite extreme we can imagine a situation in which heated moral debates are waged without those involved ever having stated precisely the fact of the case which started the whole debate. It is necessary to know exactly what is involved.

The contrast that Frankena draws between "ethical instruction" and "better knowledge of the facts" can, however, lead us astray. "Ethical instruction" is not merely the citing of "thou shalt" statements, but it implies the necessity of seeking clarity about the life situation and becoming involved in that situation. Reality is the raw material for ethics.

Acquiring factual knowledge is not a matter of random accumulation, but is a function of the reality that daily life must be lived under specific conditions. Thus the "givenness of life" includes not only the facts but also the acquiring of specific knowledge about the actual situation, thus directing the way we live in the light of the specific situations in which we find ourselves. The acquiring of factual knowledge can be carried out by mutual consultation in which knowledge of the "world" is stressed. This point of view will be encountered repeatedly and therefore will become clearer in the course of the discussion. In this initial context it has been seen that, as Frankena says, more is involved than mere knowledge of facts, that "clarity about the concepts involved" is also needed. It is thus important that the facts be accurately seen and that the judgments about what to do be made in accordance with the facts. Both work together when the discussion has as its goal the gaining of insight into the circumstances in which the question of one's own conduct arises. The answer to this question must be given in an absolute form but always in relation to the reality in which the question has arisen.

This structural element can be defined even more precisely. As we explore the data they are made to serve the purposes of our daily conduct. Thinking about such situations as the circumstances of family life, of the place where we work, or of the community in which we live brings the data into the context of daily life and serves to clarify our situation as ethical agents. In sum, what is involved is the formation of a perspective that goes beyond that of the individual and becomes part of the context in which the "external" situation and our subjective experience of that situation are united. Many moral doubts and much confusion result from lack of clarity about the actual situation in which we find ourselves.

To be sure, our analysis cannot remain static. Knowledge of the actual situation and of the relationships in which we are involved has more than a clarifying, therapeutic function. It can show us also the limits of our insights, that is, the limits of the possibility that we can fully understand, or even fully know the actual situation. Often we must lead our lives without adequate factual knowledge. And this is true not only for occasions when we do not have as much time as we would like for exploring the situation.

H. Lübbe investigated this point of view in detail and used it as the theoretical basis for a process of ethical decision making. In contrast to a "purely" theoretical process, Lübbe advanced a theory of decision making related to the specific situation, but which does not deny the possibility and necessity of knowledge of the actual context (H. Lübbe, *Theorie und Entscheidung*, 1971).

The limits of our insight into the actual situation make it all the clearer that human beings in the conduct of their lives are themselves data, that is, they are factors in the situation. It would therefore be quite incorrect to derive a theory from the first element which we have set forth here, that is, a theory according to which the goal of ethics would be to conform in each instance to what is present in the situation. That would be completely unrealistic. Instead the acquisition of data must be expanded to include one's own involvement in the actual situation.

Anyone who enters into a situation and becomes concerned with it encounters the challenge to take a stand, to become involved. The necessity of becoming oriented contains an implicit "ought." At this elementary level, "ought" is something beyond the facts of the situation as they can be discerned, but it also is a part of the situation itself. Indeed, each specific situation in life is only a section of the reality of life and can therefore be evaluated only in reference to other situations. The "ought" that emerges when we deal with specific questions of how to lead our lives speaks to our actions. As a result, knowledge of the data expands to a contextual anticipation of the connections in which the various situations are related to each other. This by no means makes the knowledge of the facts and the relationships among them superfluous. Value judgments are no substitute for such knowledge. On the contrary, extending the argument involved in structuring an ethic results in the creation of new data through further acquaintance with a specific situation, and then in something happening and changes taking place. Relationships among facts are also sequential relationships that result from dealing with situations or dealing with the results of our actions. Factual knowledge thus expands to include the question of the results of one's own actual or intended actions in a situation. Therefore reflection on the consequences of our actions is anticipation of what may really happen to the one acting as well as to others. In this way it is possible to form a preliminary picture of ethical reflection and of how this reflection is related to the given facts and the results of actions. A very tentative maxim at this point could be phrased thus: Act in such a way that you do justice to the situation in which you find yourself, and still are able to learn from the consequences of your actions. In any case, one of the givens of life is that our situation plays a role in what we do.

The conclusion which must be drawn for ethics from these observations is as follows: When we acquire knowledge of the facts, or of the relationships among them, we acquire at the same time an insight into the complexity of the factors involved, including the insight that the way we lead our own life plays a significant role. This formulation of the first element involved leads to further results. The activity which we have been describing here results in the formation of a world view, at first on a small scale. To inquire into the situation, to gain an overview of it, to consider what the results of our actions may be — these are activities that give a specific structure to the situation in which we act and that interpret it in terms of the constant factors involved in living. Extended dealing with a life situation produces a world view. Such activities are themselves expressions of the ethical reflection involved in the reality of human life, and at the same time the process by which the "ought" is present in what is. Responsibility

for our actions is not suspended in an empty space of ethical reasoning, but is developed in our on-going dealings with reality.

The next step in the argument is to affirm that ethics is always
involved in the structuring of a world view. When the discussion is
pushed to this point it is easy to object that any dealing with the facts
of the situation, yes, even knowledge of the facts, has been determined by the world view with which we set out. That is quite true.
But it is also a theoretical conclusion which is based on the analysis
of the actual reality of our acts. It is not an objection that could
justify us in assuming that a world view would come into being on
its own without the necessity of our dealing with the actual life situation. Therefore the specific manner in which we deal with reality
must first be examined in the light of whether this presupposition is
accurate, and if so, how. It is not advisable for an ethicist to regard
ethics as merely an exposition of world views, or to begin with such
an exposition. The very origin of a world view involves and is determined by experience, especially by experiences that include complex
life situations. Thus the formation of a world view is not only and not
primarily the result of the pressure of a specific situation that calls
for actions. But neither can our world view be maintained in isolation from the way we lead our lives. It is shaped more or less explicitly
in the discourse of everyday life and has as its pervasive, general
theme the whole of the reality of life. And this in turn is built up out
of its specific elements.

This brings us to the limits of what can be learned from this first
closer examination of the issue. But one more important question
must be considered. The differences among various specific ethical
formulations are closely involved with the degree to which the task
of constructing a world view is comprehended. There are also
specialized ethics, the ethics of a profession, of family, of politics, of
a community. They take on their special shape because they are
related to the experiences of a specific life context. Their scope is
quite limited. Therefore they are not mutually exclusive, even though
they are the occasion of conflicts among the various life situations. By
contrast we can imagine an ethic that is concerned with all of
humanity and the whole of human life, and which therefore develops
a world view that takes into consideration the basic situation of life.
But even such a "general" ethic cannot simply be applied directly to
all possible or actual situations. This multiplicity of ethical world
views creates difficulties for the formation of ethical theories, but

these can easily be explained when we keep in mind the connection between ethics and actual situations and experiences. Theological ethics has similar characteristics in that it has a tradition of specialized ethics of family, state, and so forth, as well as the tradition of a general ethic, whose relationship to specalized ethics must be discussed anew in each case. Beyond this similarity, the distinctive nature of a theological ethic is that it establishes a world view that seeks to encompass the reality of human life in such a manner as to do justice to the actual givenness of life as life that humans have received from God. But in saying this we anticipate the further methodological course of the discussion.

2) From the Recognition of Ethical Presuppositions to the Formation of Tradition

"It is only because what is historically present is there without our effort and because we can build on it that our efforts have any chance of success. No human being can make an absolutely new beginning, but each must start with what is already there. The future needs the heritage of the past" (O. Marquand in W. Oelmüller, *Philosophische Arbeitsbücher* 2, 1977, p. 14).

Anyone who faces the question of what should be done must also ask what presuppositions must be heeded and respected, and what cautions must be observed in reference to the possible outcome of human actions. The perception of facts and the construction of a world view that establishes relationships among the facts includes a history in which humans come to self-awareness by living their lives. Thus the next step in the methodological construction of ethics is to explicate the structure of the formation of ethical tradition. The reflective nature of ethics is especially evident when we direct our attention to the historical nature of a specific ethic. One of the facts relevant to ethics is that each specific ethic does, indeed must, take into account the standards and traditions developed in history. The establishment of an ethically relevant world view does not occur in an ethically neutral realm but is determined by the existing ethical culture.

The explanation and description of an ethical culture is the theme of moral doctrine. They are part of the prehistory of modern empirical sociology, of which H. Schelsky has said that it is the "social historiography of the present day" (H. Schelsky, *Ortsbestimmung der Soziologie*, 1959, p. 74).

The question of the relationship of ethics and history is a part of the theory of scientific ethics. The relation in content and method arises because history is a complex of human events. An ethic that is concerned with elementary principles and with claims to validity must always be aware that the "Sitz im Leben" of ethics is constituted by these specific and distinctive factors which are the givens in the conduct of life. This touches on a theme that played a dominant role in Schleiermacher's ethics: "Ethics is determined by history." For it seeks to bring out the universal of human life in the specifics, and thus must include "the knowledge of the specific." Therefore "nothing can be expressed in ethics except to the extent to which it is expressed in history" (*Ethik* 1816. General introduction to *Entwürfe zu einem System der Sittenlehre*, ed. O. Braun, reprinted 1967, *Schleiermachers Werke*, vol. 2, p. 499). Schleiermacher expressed the relationship between ethics and history in the formula, "History is the picture book of ethical teaching, and ethical teaching is the book of formulas for history" (ibid., p. 549). On Schleiermacher's thought, see H. J. Birkner, *Schleiermachers christliche Sittenlehre im Zusammenhang seines philosophisch-theologischen Systems*, 1964).

The systematic interest in the historical nature of ethics that inheres in the discussion of morality and conduct and of their development is itself an interest in reality. It is concerned with the question of how the responsibilities explored by ethical theory can be brought into the actual relationships of life and how the conduct of life can be given a structure that goes beyond the individual. This interest must also be included in the study of ethics, so that "ethical instruction" (Frankena) can be more than and different from instruction about subjective intentions and the chance position of the teacher.

For his understanding of the historical formation of ethical reality, Hegel employed the concept of *morality*, (*Sittlichkeit*), in which he included the historical institutions "in which morality and convictions express themselves in actions and attain reality in the unity of the objective and the subjective," J. Ritter in his article "Ethik VI" in the *Historisches Wörterbuch der Philosophie*, vol. 2, 1972, p. 792. In addition, reference may be made to Ritter's extremely important Hegel studies brought together in *Metaphysik und Politik. (Studien zu Aristoteles und Hegel*, 1969).

In reality the concept of "institution" is well suited to express the relationship of the actual reality of life and the way life is currently lived. Institutions are neither "pure" theory nor "pure" empirical reality, but constitute an ethical reality of their own, the formation of traditions, both as carrying traditions forward and as renewing them.

On the theory of the institution, see also W. Korff, "Instutions-theorie," in *Handbuch der christlichen Ethik*, vol. 1, 1978, pp. 168ff.

In the context of this argument the critical objection arises that actions guided by the past are based only on historical reasons and supported only by social conventions. This historical objection, which is also expressed as the objection to conventionalism, is current everywhere and derives its relevance for the practical issues of life from the relationship of the generations to each other, that is to say, it is the critical objection raised in each generation by the "young" against their "elders" and already had its own tradition in the relationship of one generation to the other. But its relevance is also more generally based on the experiences of social and historical change which make traditional orientations and institutions seem outmoded, at least in the sense that they are no longer able to deal adequately with contemporary life. This objection can also be raised against an entire tradition, as for example, globally against the whole history of Christianity.

Any ethic that appealed only to traditions and conventions would indeed be completely inadequate if that ethic relied on externally given and externally maintained authorities for the conduct of life. But the criticism of tradition has as its goal the identification and critical adaptation of the bases for the constitution of a historical form of ethics or a moral way of life.

The demand for such criticism is above all connected with the name of K. Popper, whose critical rationalism is closely involved with a highly ethical claim that all existing norms and the basis on which they stand should be examined. Popper's book, *The Open Society and its Enemies* (1944, 1950), is especially important for an understanding of the ethical position of critical rationalism. Popper's position is expressly upheld by H. Albert in his *Traktat über kritische Vernunft*, 2d ed., 1969, esp. pp. 29ff. and 55ff.

The historical objection can appeal to Kant's criticism that only that which proceeds from a human being's own autonomous decision on rational grounds and on the basis of freedom can be an ethical judgment or an ethically based action. In the methodological course of our investigation this objection calls our attention to the question of whether there is a necessary contradiction between ethical tradition and an independent basis for the conduct of one's own life. This question will now be explored by examining the following premise: An ethic always implies the formation of a tradition.

In the interests of enlivening the discussion by a change of approach, I will now follow a line of argument inspired by acquaintance with analytical philosophy. It can be developed out of the following observation: Anyone who decides to accept specific value judgments also decides actually to carry them out in specific cases. This is a decision to accept and recognize them as presuppositions for one's actions. It is also a decision for a certain consistency of action, and not only for a subjective acceptance of value judgments. It is also, we might say, a decision for a sort of tradition of one's own actions and not for acting first one way and then another. The actions are oriented to specific standards. Anyone committed to act morally is also committed to specific presuppositions. They make it possible to act according to rational points of view, and for this approach it is not decisive whether or not the value judgments are themselves based on rational grounds. The question of the theoretical justification of ethical judgments raises quite different problems. See below, pp. 153–55.

The standards constitute the point of reference for ethical reflection in that in relation to them we can identify contradictions in one's actual conduct. The significant point is that moral action is distinguished from arbitrary and capricious activity by being tied to presuppositions, in relation to which it can be subject to self-evaluation. This leads to the formation of a tradition in an individual case. This formation makes possible a certain consistency in life and a reflectivity that can form judgments.

In the case of the formation of such an individual tradition, we can also speak of the development of a way of life. A way of life includes a specific world view, that is, the perception that life is lived in a specific way. The formation of ethical judgments itself constitutes a way of life, that is, it establishes presuppositions which guide actions in detail and the conduct of life as a whole. Consistency of action means also that actions can be repeated according to intelligible and known points of view.

A similar line of argument can be derived from the position represented by C. L. Stevenson (*Ethic and Language*, 1941) in relation to R. M. Hare (*The Language of Morals*, 1952). See also E. v. Savigny, *Die Philosophie der normalen Sprache*, 1969, pp. 169ff.

The result of this line of thought is that the critical objection to tradition cannot in principle be accepted in any case for the structure of ethics. Rather, we must say, an ethic always implies a tradition. To be sure this does not preclude the scrutiny of specific traditions, but rather leaves the way open for it. The critic must go to the pains of formulating a specific negation. The right to criticize tradition cannot be asserted in a general and sweeping manner. Therefore the fact that a person is acting and living on the basis of a historically constructed heritage does not justify the a priori suspicion that that person is acting only according to convention and not for good moral reasons. The reconstruction of what we mean by the answer of ethical tradition leads to the conclusion that the establishment of traditions is a necessary step in the process of forming ethical judgments. And if this is true, it is true not only for one's "own" individual case, but also for already developed standards and ways of life. The formation of tradition as reconstructed with reference to the individual case can thus be extended to the reconstruction of this structural element in ethics. Even though this does not produce any specific decisions as to content, it is at least possible to insist that ethical tradition is not, merely because it is tradition, predestined to be critically dissolved and altered.

In reference to this last mentioned problem, Hermann Lübbe formulated the rule of the burden of proof. It goes like this: In the case of a demand for new standards which affect the way we lead our lives and the institutions that undergird us, it is not the existing tradition that bears the burden of proof for this own correctness, but whoever sets up the new rules. First of all we can assume that the existing standards are valid because they have proved themselves, something we do not yet know about the newly proposed standards or rules (H. Lübbe, "Traditionsverlust und Fortschrittskrise," in *Fortschritt als Orientierungsproblem*, 1971, p. 343).

This argument also says that the ethical traditions themselves have become a practical form for ethical discourse about life. Thus they are in themselves an argument for their continuation.

That ethics involves history is seen also when we look at the finitude of our human life and the limited capacity of each individual to engage in ethical reflection. Thus N. Luhmann can say that our using history as a basis for our actions is urgently necessary, because our own finite capacity is too limited for us to build upon it general bases for actions, that is, to create a situation in which we could act (N. Luhmann, "Evolution und Geschichte," in *Soziologische Aufklärung* 2 (1975): 150–69).

But the relationship of ethics and history involves also an essentially constructive feature. Therefore the argument must in conclusion be formulated as follows: Anyone who acts morally must affirm an ethical tradition and be involved in the construction of such a tradition. That is the point that brings us to the discussion of an additional structural element in ethics.

3) From Dependence to Freedom: The World as Society

"The biography of an individual is from the moment of birth the history of relations with others" (Peter L. Berger, Sociology. A Biographical Approach, 1972).

"We share with others the reality of the everyday world" (Peter Berger and Thomas Luckmann, The Social Construction of Reality, 1966, p. 28). The obvious banality of these statements makes us aware that the world is already constituted as a social entity prior to any specific actions, intentions, or obligations. "The social structure of reality" formulates an experience of reality, the theoretical point of which is the concept of a reality of the world, independent of any subject, as a social reality.

Sociology instead of ethics? This reduces to a slogan the question of the emphasis on basic elements of ethics as an emphasis on elements of the crisis in ethics. If we replace the question mark with an exclamation point, we call attention to a trend of that formation of theory in the social sciences that undertakes objectification as the programmatic de-subjectifying of the specifically human social world. The dominant epistomological interest is then to identify structural elements and regularities of society that are independent of any subjectivity, and which would be able to explain the nature of the challenge with which reality confronts us. Sociology is the especially pregnant and prominent form of the "search for reality" that grew out of the uncertainty of modern ethical subjectivity and seeks for other, objective criteria for what is valid and thus should be valid.

Auf der Suche nach Wirklichkeit (the search for reality) is the characteristic title of a book by the sociologist H. Schelsky, 1965.

The basic premise, an ethic always implies a social world, is, however, open to differing interpretations. For ethical discussion it says first of all that an ethic cannot be developed out of the actions of a subject, but that in terms of social reality it lays claim on the human person. To put it briefly, ethics is above all social ethics.

This corresponds in a certain way to the understanding of the ethical task in Reformation theology. It dealt concretely with ethics in the doctrine of office and calling and of the various status levels and ordinances. A renewal and transformation of this still precritical social ethics of given institutions (precritical means not yet influenced by the debate with modern critical sociology) would mean conceiving of social ethics in a specifically modern understanding of society and not understanding it simply as applied individual ethics. In contrast to the less than real abstract individual, the concept of society promises a fuller and richer concept of reality.

E. Troeltsch's great study, *Die Soziallehren der christlichen Kirchen und Gruppen*, 1910, *Gesammelte Werke*, vol. 1, 1965, was the product of the critique of a naive understanding of social ethics as was seen, for example, in its identification with the "social question" at the end of the nineteenth century. Troeltsch turned around the question of what the church could do for the social question, and "applied the entire sociological questioning to the total history of Christianity." It would be incorrect to assert that theological ethics has caught up with, much less surpassed, the claims of the program which Troeltsch proposed and then executed.

For the new orientation of ethics as social ethics under the influence of modern social sciences, the work of H. D. Wendland is especially important. In particular, attention should be called to his essay, "Das Verständnis der heutigen Gesellschaft in der evangelischen Soziallehre," in *Botschaft an die soziale Welt*, 1959, pp. 166–76, and to his programmatic book, *Die Kirche in der modern Gesellschaft*, 1956. One of the important early contributions to this concern for a new theoretical approach of social ethics is his article, "Soziale Verantwortung in der säkularisierten Gesellschaft," ZEE 7 (1963): 72ff, especially the section, 'Zur sozialethischen Definition der Gesellschaft.' The ethics of G. Winter grew out of an intensive debate with the social sciences, *Elements for a Social Ethic*, 1966.

The new approach oriented to sociology poses an important methodological problem. How does ethics gain access to reality? Would not a theory of society independent of any subject mean the end of ethics? The continuing work of defining the task of ethics will be served by taking as an example the construction of ethics from the point of view of sociology. It is not possible or desirable to take into account the whole breadth of contemporary sociology. The explosion of theoretical and empirical studies makes that impossible in any case. We will concentrate exclusively on the question how the social element as basic to the structure of ethics can be described in sociological terms in such a way as to make possible a broader access to ethical investigation. The premise that an ethic always implies a social world can be qualified as follows: Reality proceeds from interaction, and whatever proceeds from interaction is then "society as objective reality" (Berger/Luckmann, pp. 49ff.). It is this "objective reality" that we are dealing with when we attempt to determine methodologically what ethics is. Objectivity is a relative concept, that is, it is always relative to a subject. Precedence must be given to this point.

Because of its relevance for ethics the question of the objectivity of sociology as a science is acute. This question was raised in the well-known treatment given the subject by M. Weber, *Die "Objektivität" sozialwissenschaftlicher Erkenntnis*, 1904. It has recently stirred up a major interdisciplinary debate, the so-called "Positivism Debate." See Th. W. Adorno et al., ed., *Der Positivismusstreit in der deutschen Soziologie*, 1969.

Objectivity is another term for independence of the subject. Is an ethic that is independent of a subject conceivable at all? Before we judge too quickly we must examine more closely some elements of the matter to be clarified. As has often been emphasized, ethics represents a specific interest in reality, that is, an interest not merely to formulate subjective observations and questions of what is right, but to make certain of the relationship of ethics to reality. This motif could also derive support from sociology, but not from it alone.

Thus P. Althaus spoke of a "basis of the commandments in reality," so that the moral restraints on humanity could be spoken of. Yet this is obviously a reality "for us" and thus not without relation to a subject. In the context of this discussion Althaus spoke of ethics as a "biology of a higher order" (*Grundriss der Ethik*, 1953, pp. 27, 30). Along this line there developed also the attempt to define ethics by the term "ethology." O. Ritschl attempted to introduce this concept into Protestant ethics, but he did not meet with acceptance (*Ethology*, 3 vols., 1899). Only in behavioral studies did the term ethology find a settled home as the study of animal society. From there it has exerted influence on ethics by way of behavioral studies. It was in this sense that a pupil of Konrad Lorenz, W. Wickler developed a biological ethics, *Die Biologie der 10 Gebote*, 1971.

Instead of this, it would be easy to speak of ethics as a "sociology of a higher order." Recent anthropological research has built very productive bridges between biology and sociology. Helmut Plessner (*Die Stufen des Organischen und der Mensch*, [1928], 1975) and

Arnold Gehlen (*Der Mensch. Seine Natur und Seine Stellung in der Welt*, 1940, 1966) have had wide influence in this area.

Gehlen derived the anthropological conditions that lead to the formation of a socio-cultural nature of humankind from the fact that humans, as biological beings, are unfinished. Their physical and organic endowment, especially the structure of their drives, is nonspecific, that is, it does not determine humanity. This is the essential biological difference from the rest of nature, especially the animal world. But therefore, in Gehlen's interpretation, life itself is a task for humans. In order to live they must create a world for themselves. The socio-cultural world is the biologically necessary creation of humanity. The world of society is necessary to life. In order to live, humans need a second, socio-cultural birth. Society is not something added to "finished" humans, but is essential to their survival.

With these and related theories, especially the separation or distinction between human subjectivity and the objective world in which we live, the focus is shifted to the world of life, and at the same time human dependence on society occupies the foreground. With a certain theoretically based compulsion, human freedom is subsumed under society. As a consequence it might be said that sociology is a higher form of human ethics. For it perceives those conditions for the conduct of life that are objective, independent of any subject, necessary, and social. Even this objective social nature still includes the necessity of taking a position in reference to the conduct of one's own life. In the writings of Karl Marx, the source of the strongest impulses for studying the social aspects of humanity, the theory of society largely takes the place of ethics. In his early writings he developed the thesis that the true nature of humankind is its social nature (Karl Marx, *Die Frühschriften*, ed. S. Landshut, 1955).

Research into the historical laws by which society develops has taken over the task of forming links with the concept of an ethic. On the basis of a historical and materialistic theory of society, an ethic that is oriented to a moral individual appears as the outgrowth of a deterministic economic context, because the formation of our social nature through work is an economic process. The historical regularity of the process of society assumes the role of the ethical subject. An ethic in an express sense can according to Marxist theory become a theme when the sure consciousness of the course of the history of society recedes. That is the case in so-called revisionism. Or on the other hand, the status of social development is so advanced that it appears

possible to formulate an ethic that corresponds to an objective historical reality of society as incorporation of individuals into the objective
status of a socialistic society. That is the case in recent Marxist ethics.

A glimpse of the ethical discussion in orthodox Marxism is given by the
volume, *Philisophisch-ethiscke Forschungen in der Sowjetunion*, ed. A. G.
Chartschew and R. Miller, 1976. Informative for the discussion in "western"
Marxism is the book, *Moral und Gesellschaft*, with contributions by K.
Kosik, J. P. Sartre, C. Luporini, R. Garaudy and others, 1968.

In the Marxist approach, what role is played by the conduct of
human life? The relationship between ethics and society, which is still
controversial in Marxist theory, is connected with the historical
character of the theory of society. In this the critique of the individual
has an ethical dimension, which goes beyond the historical dimension
of the theory of society. Marx developed his theory on the model of
the individual subject as an egoist, and therefore the history of capi-
tal could provide him with the key to the reality of society. For the
economic determinism of society is at its core its conditioning by
egoistic interests. The assumption that this egoism of the isolated
individual subject would be overcome by the transformation of the
economic means of production, that is, by the socialization of the
means of production, depends on the other assumption that our
social nature is our true human nature. The claim of oughtness which
this theory contains leads by its own logic to the conclusion that
everything is economically determined. But it is no longer able to
explain how humans, conditioned economically by their social
nature, can become the subjects of these conditions in order to alter
them, and therefore how we are to conceive of freedom in relation
to society. Therefore Marxist theory is bound in its practice to end up
with the subordination of humans to a specific historical order of
society, because it cannot of itself hold itself open to its own critique.

The distinguishing structural features of our social nature are not
identical with the historical character of a specific development of
society. Instead, when we consider any specific society, the thesis that
humanity is not fully expressed in that which exists at present, not
even in its social nature, is valid.

Thus the relationship between ethics and sociology is not to be
found in the alternative of individual or society, any more than freedom is the opposite of the social nature of humans. Freedom includes
social dependence, but the specific, historically identifiable depen-
dencies are not the ultimately valid definition of human sociality.

Other discoveries are also possible in reference to our social nature. An elementary sociological observation reminds us that a human being always lives in a plurality of social worlds. "It can be said that in our experience of society we dwell at the same time in differing worlds" (Peter Berger, *Sociology*, 1974, p. 14). Social nature becomes a proper theme of ethics, because we do not live in only "one" world. Plurality and complexity are thus highly significant concepts for understanding our social nature. They perform a critical function in relation to all concepts of "one" society that seek to give to society the unambiguous meaning of a transindividual subject. If this plurality is deemed a contradiction of "bourgeois" society and traced back to economically determined interests, then the moral demand is to erect "one" society, the realization of which will be the realization of "one" humanity, "man" as a category. A pluralistic society is then regarded as defective. This critique pursues the goal of bringing about the historical identity of humanity and society. Pluralism must then be combatted as the negation of human freedom in the interests of dependence on society. The struggle against human individuality, however, becomes also the struggle against the individuality of each specific social structure.

On the other hand, the basic elements of pluralism and complexity in society correspond to the basic element of human individuality as freedom in relation to society, in contrast to an abstract individual. Individuality is the ethical concept of freedom in the perspective of the social nature of the world.

The biologically oriented sociology of A. Gehlen is also hostile to pluralism, because it endeavors to understand human social nature entirely in terms of the model of the stable environment of an animal society. Thus in a conservative manner it ends up in a criticism of ethics which, as a criticism of pluralism, is structurally similar to Marxist sociology.

This is especially clear in Gehlen's last book, *Moral und Hypermoral*, 1969, in which, in spite of the misleading subtitle "A Pluralistic Ethic," only the contrast between individualism and power finds expression. Pluralism is for Gehlen only the obscuring of power, on which all depends.

The sociological discussion has not brought about the end of ethics but its renewal. This is seen clearly in the renewal of practical philosophy (see below, pp. 169–77). Here special attention should be directed to a point of view that contributes to further precision in the basic elements of ethics set forth here. The sociological thesis that reality is the product of interaction has been made to bear fruit for the question of the interpersonal nature of ethics. The line of argument is as follows: The validity of ethical norms for actions cannot simply be assumed in the sense of their having substantiality. It is not enough to evoke a norm in an individual case. Rather, norms are valid interpersonally only when they rest on an interpersonal basis, that is, a social basis. The reality of ethics is the reality of a community of communication. Ethics is built up in a social process, in a communication network. But the establishing of a communication network that is suited to establishing interpersonally valid norms involves a readiness, a commitment to a world in which the social nature of ethics plays a role. This readiness must itself be independent of the success or failure of a process of ethical communication. Otherwise ethical social relations would be permanently threatened by the collapse of communication. It must be able to count on continuity, and this implies a previous achievement, which can be formulated as the readiness to affirm a world in which we function.

4) *From the Givenness of the World to the Affirmation of Reality*

"If a person who honors the moral law and entertains the thought (which he can scarcely avoid doing) of what world he would create, guided by practical reason, if it were in his power to do so, and create in such a way as to include himself as a participant in it, he would not merely choose it in such a way as to bring with it the moral idea of the highest good, if the choice were left to him, but he would also will that a world should exist . . ." (Kant, *Religion Within the Limits of Reason Alone*, preface to the first edition).

Consensus does not protect us against error. The task of ethics is not exhausted in the structure of a communication community. The social nature of rules of consensus does not have the final word in the structure of ethics. Not every agreement that is aimed for by way of communication is an adequate foundation for ethics. The question remains what it is that we seek agreement about. Ethics as an action of communication must be directed toward a goal of action.

In order for an action to qualify as "good," the question must be considered, "what then will be the result of this action of ours?" (Kant, op. cit.). It is necessary to think about the final goal, the "success" of our action. That is the question which gives to a duty ethic its particular place in ethical discussion. What is at issue here?

A community of communication and the formation of a consensus are not ends in themselves. The success of actions always has significance for them. Therefore we carry the specifying of the structural elements of ethics further, in that we apply the results of the discussion of the previously considered three points to ethics itself. Kant phrased the issue thus: Anyone who asks what it means to do good is also asking "what world he would like to see created under the guidance of practical reason," if that were in his power. This is an important control question that can protect us against moral dreaming and phantasies far removed from reality. The method by which this control is applied to oneself is to imagine a world "in which you could place yourself as a participant," thus a world which involves us and is relevant to us. But this can only be a world that can be realized under certain circumstances, to which we ourselves belong, to whose realization we can contribute as the persons we are, and in which we ourselves are willing to live.

The goal toward which Kant's speculative argument moves is that an ethic always implies the construction or creation of a world. For ethics does not consist merely in intentions, but involves the bringing of something to pass, with the success of our actions. This, however, involves the consequence that anyone who desires the good must also desire a world in which that good reigns. This speculative reconstruction of the relationship of ethics to reality involves a number of important specific features that can make the line of thought clear.

First, if the consequences of our actions, their success, is a constituent part of ethics, then the classic question of moral theology arises anew: What is the connection between the intention to do the good, and one's own well being? In traditional terminology it is the question of the connection between the duty to do the good and our happiness. There must be some relationship here. In any case the assumption is not very convincing that we could regard the outcome of our acts as good if it turns out badly for us. But it does not make sense to imagine actions without any consequences.

Such a pure ethic of intentions, oriented solely to the purity of our intentions and forbidden to reflect on the result of our actions, or their usefulness, would be a distortion of ethics, even if it were meant well. It could no longer be corrected by the question of the purpose and the consequences of our actions.

A pure doctrine of success, which honored the maxim that the end justifies the means would be just as aberrant. If I achieve only my own well being, regardless of the means I use, then duty has nothing more to say to the question of success.

Under empirical conditions, however, we do not have at our command the capability of attaining in every case, or even in any case, an agreement of duty and happiness. We have no certainty of being able to bring about such agreement. The experiences of every life demonstrate this. This discrepancy can lead to an ethical dualism. It might take the form that one would affirm an ethical duty only for a world that could guarantee success and happiness, a "whole" world in which moral intention and ethical reality were in harmony. Otherwise ethical duty would be ignored in the face of a specific world.

This position can be phrased as a principle, which would then read, That which exists is always evil (E. Bloch, *Das Prinzip Hoffnung*, 1959). Only a different, future, possible world, a "good" world, could be a reality to which we were bound by duty. That results in a corruption of ethics by the expectation of happiness, even when it is elevated eschatologically. The result is a moralism without ethical seriousness.

The difference of which we are speaking here is the content of an experience of empirical humanity, which informs us of our capability, or incapability, of constructing a world in which both duty and happiness are certain. In this situation of practical experience all that empirical humans have at their command is the element of duty. Duty does not tie us to the difference identified above, but instead it orients us to activity that is directed toward success, to the relationship of ethics to reality.

From this it follows that ethics always implies an unconditional yes to reality, the acceptance of the world in which we live. By this the principle of reality becomes binding on ethics, that is, it becomes a duty that must be observed even in the face of the difference between what ought to be and what is, and that protects us from avoiding the given reality in a gnostic-dualistic manner. In other words, anyone who acknowledges duties only when success is guaranteed, is making a principle of ethics out of something that humans do not have control over. Such a morality generates a hatred of reality, a wellspring of aggression against the world or other persons who stand in the way of one's own happiness. This would be to sacrifice the indicative of ethics as an offering to an imperative totally divorced from reality.

Only those who can speak an unconditional yes to reality can expect in a specific case and a specific manner to be able to achieve good. By contrast, a yes with reservations makes the success of one's actions from the outset dependent on a self-defined world. But the yes to reality is in the nature of an accomplishment that defines duty as taking up one's own duty.

A practical consequence of the unconditional yes to reality as the acceptance of the world of human beings is the capacity to compromise. The ethical structure of compromise involves the intention to achieve, within the realm of the desired final goal, an attainable success. It takes into account the situation that those involved in the action do not have absolute capabilities, but only capabilities that are mutually limiting. A conscious compromise is one that remains aware of its nature as compromise. We remain thus aware only when we see it in relationship to the "good," as the idea of the harmony between duty and happiness. In a certain sense a compromise chooses the "mean" because it incorporates the affirmation of the reality of actions into the intention of the one acting.

W. Trillhaas devoted attention to compromise as an important category of ethics in his article, "Zum Problem des Kompromisses," ZEE 4 (1960): 355ff. For an understanding of the Aristotelian category of "mean," see the major work of G. Bien, *Die Grundlegung der politischen Philosophie bei Aristoteles*, 1973.

To be sure, an approach of this sort that advocates an unconditional yes to reality includes a theological argument. Kant's argument is also the reformulation of a basic theological concept. He wrote, "Morality . . . leads inescapably to religion, which expands it to the idea of a powerful, moral Lawgiver, outside mankind, whose will includes the final goal of the creation, which can and should also be the final goal of mankind" (op. cit., p. 652).

For an interpretation of Kant's writing on religion see the recent work of H. Renz, *Geschichtsgedanke und Christusfrage. Zur Christusanschauung Kants und deren Fortbildung durch Hegel im Hinblick auf die allgemeine Funktion neuzeitlicher Theologie*, 1977.

The ethical postulate of a concept of God has a mediating function between the general nature of the ethical principle of reality and the specific nature of the given human reality. It is this relationship to God that frees us to see the individuality of human action, but in such a way that the universality of the reality of ethical duty can be maintained.

5) *From the Human World to God's Creation*

"And God saw everything that he had made, and behold, it was very good" (Gen. 1:31). This final word from the first creation story of the Old Testament gives rise to ironic reformulation when we think of it as applied to man: "And man saw everything that he had made, and behold, perhaps his intentions were good, but the results were devastating."

In the theological tradition, accepting the world as God's creation has been the stimulus to two thoroughly contradictory results. On the one hand, to remember that the world is here because God created it can lead us to develop the theme of the difference between human actions and capabilities and God's original will for the created world. This difference then finds expression in the idea of sin and human guilt, which develops its own dynamic for salvation history and moves toward the conclusion that "The World Must be Healed Through Humanity," to cite the title of a book by E. Steinbach, *Die Welt muss in Menschen Heil Werden,* 1963. This takes place through redemption and reconciliation, and the road leads from creation to Christology.

On the other hand, in remembering the creation, the perception of this difference can take as its theme the contemporary reality of the meaning of creation as resistance against human sin, and then emphasize the limits of the power of human wrongs. We then are pointed to the condition of the world as creation, which in spite of human sin gives scope to ethical thought that is capable of producing renewal. Thus the doctrine of creation contains within it a key theological function which in this century has led to a theological quarrel about basics. Therefore if we speak of the creaturely nature of humankind we must also speak of the world as creation. In the context of an analysis of the basic elements of ethics we must deal with the various possible answers that have been offered by the ethical tradition. This involves setting them forth precisely in a manner that allows a specific theological dimension to emerge. To proceed methodologically we can use the formula of H. Ringeling that ethics is the discipline of integration.

Ringeling developed this formula in outline in his essay, "Ethik als Integrationswissenschaft" (1974), reprinted in *Ethik vor der Sinnfrage,* 1980, pp. 113ff. In more carefully worked out form it is found in the *Handbuch der christlichen Ethik,* vol. 1, 1978, Part III, pp. 389ff.

If we pursue the second alternative, the theological interest centers on the understanding of the world as God's world, according to which there is something that strongly resists human sin. The theological intention can be easily explained. Human sin cannot be regarded as having the power to make the will and work of God the Creator of no effect. The world must, even in the case of human sin, preserve a significance of creation that is superior to sin. The world cannot and must not be thought of as atheistic. This significance, however, cannot be fully expressed in terms of human intentions and attitudes. It must on the contrary be thought of as relatively independent of the subjective human condition. The theological meaning of the world as God's creation is a challenge that addresses humans out of the created world and asserts itself even against the distorted meaning of mankind. In this connection the idea of creation functions in ethics as the theme of resistance against the sinful will of humanity. The composition of the world as created world expresses itself in such ethical phenomena as cause humans to do good, contrary to their own selfish will. It is not human moral or religious intentionality that guides persons to act in accord with creation, but this is imposed on humanity from "outside" by the world. The goodness of the world as creation, as God's world, is not conditioned by the moral quality of the human beings who are acting within it. It has its own rules, to which humans must submit, sometimes under compulsion. Above all else the ethical significance of the concept of creation is that it deals with the conflict between the goodness of creation and the evil of human actions in and to the world. If we take this conflict as the substantive basis for the conflict between what is and what ought to be, then it is clear that the appeal to the significance of the world as creation renews with one theological argument the unity of what is and what ought to be in terms of the givenness of the world as God's creation. Then it also follows that under these circumstances humans are not addressed as ethicists of intention, but are confronted by the actual demands of their worldly existence.

This is precisely the point which led to the concept of ordinances of creation as factors of an objective, reality-oriented ethic.

An explicit "theology of ordinances" is something new. It found expression especially in the writings of P. Althaus, who in 1935 published a study under this title.

H.-W. Schütte, wrote a brief but very informative critical introduction to the theology of ordinances: *Theologie der Ordnung, Gesellschaftlische Herausforderung des Christentums*, ed. W. Schmidt, 1969, pp. 59–68. H. Thielicke made extensive use of the idea of creation ordinances, and interpreted them chiefly as "emergency ordinances" (H. Thielicke, *Theologische Ethik* I, 3d ed., 1965, p. 609).

Even though reference to human sin is important for our understanding of the ordinances as "external" ordinances, the ethical significance of the ordinances of creation should not be reduced to the argument from human sin. Indeed, according to Lutheran doctrinal tradition, under these conditions the ordinances bring into play the reality of the goodness of God's creation.

The distinctive nature of the ordinances of creation as ethical structural elements is seen in that they lay claim to humans through their positive, specific, and factual nature. They are ethically binding, not because of the particular nature of ordinances, but because of their actual, empirical validity. The reason for this is enlightening. When the human ethical sense is corrupted by sin, this corruption also affects the attempts to specify a human essence. The binding nature of the world as a good creation of God must therefore present itself as an external ordinance, that is as a positive, established ordinance. At this point the ethical doctrine of ordinances coincides with the tradition of the Aristotelian and medieval doctrine of rank as a doctrine of ordinances that are preordained for humanity. If the binding ethical authority of the world as creation cannot be established by the ethical significance of the human subject, it must be established by the data provided by established, external authorities. Nonetheless, we must ask critically whether this outcome is contained in the logic of the theological argument, as is implied in the history of this doctrine.

The connection of the doctrine of ordinances with the traditional doctrine of ranks later became a source of misunderstanding and ambiguity. It gave the impression that the ordinances of creation were identical with a specific, social, and historical society of rank of the pre-modern world, while all changes in ordinances were then to be blamed on the sinfulness of humanity. This secondary, but very influential conservatism of the doctrine of ordinances made it possible to obscure its theological and ethical significance. If we set aside the political lines drawn over the issue, which gave to Lutheranism the reputation of a merely conservative social ethic, the main theological problem that arose from the combining of these positions is that "a relationship was posited between God and humanity similar to that between two earthly ranks" (Schütte, op. cit., p. 65). This obscured the dimension of a renewal of the meaning of creation that goes beyond isolated, historical ordinances.

Previous discussions of the "answer of ethical tradition" have thus, by returning to the structural elements of the ethical tradition, tended to escape from this dilemma, and by opening up a fundamental perspective, to attain new access to the theological basis of ethics in the doctrine of creation. It is important to mention those structural elements which must be recognized as presupposed by any construction of an ethic, even though specific ordinances can always be recognized as human creations.

This tendency is also found in some sense in the new program of a "theology of ordinances" insofar as it imposes a theological theory that allows itself "to be shaped by the openness of Christianity to human self-consciousness" (Schütte, op. cit., p. 60). This could constitute a program for overcoming the crisis of theology which, under the influence of secular human consciousness, let itself be misled into a christological reductionism, and therefore was threatened with the loss of an independent Christian ethic (cf. the discussion in Part I above, pp. 16–18).

The appeal to the ordinances of creation bears a certain similarity to the Catholic doctrine of natural law. Reformation theology built directly on the Christian natural law of the Middle Ages. The point of difference that led to natural law becoming an issue of sectarian dispute was and is the point where the program of natural law claimed that humans could have knowledge of the essence of the moral ordinances, which as objects of rational knowledge claimed the same status as the knowledge revealed through Christ, and thus natural law and grace were reduced to the same epistemological level. Here the protest raised by the Lutheran doctrine of justification of necessity led to a criticism, which while continuing to recognize a functional natural law, as later developed in the liberal natural law thought of the seventeenth century, relegated theological knowledge derived from natural law to a quite different status. The Catholic doctrine of natural law has now, under the influence of the historical nature of all law, undergone an extensive revision of its philosophical and theological premises, so that this old sectarian dispute is today largely irrelevant.

For information on this issue, see A. Hertz, "Das Naturrecht," in *Handbuch der christlichen Ethik*, vol. 1, 1978, pp. 317–38. See also the bibliography on pp. 34–35.

In conclusion, a specific question that is beginning to attract considerable attention may be examined briefly. In the context of the ecological debate the question has arisen as to how far the doctrine of creation makes it necessary to distinguish between the world as given to mankind in its natural state, and the world as it has been structured and formed by human technology and science. Another question is whether the world as creation is to be equated with a natural world, untouched by civilization. The answer must be no, if nature and creation are to be taken as absolute equivalents. The reason is that what is said of the world as creation should, since it is theological discourse, set forth the idea that the world, both as the world of humanity and the natural world, does not simply exist in and of itself, but is the result of a will that manifests itself in the *creatio continua* as the continuous creative activity of God. This activity, however, includes and lays claim to the nature of humans as subjects. The "dominion over the earth" conferred in Genesis 1 can by no means be used to serve a life style bound to nature. And this is not claimed by any informed reflective thought on ecology and ethics.

The negation of the human role as subject in relation to and in contrast to nature is in truth the negation of specific consequences of human dominance over nature. The result of the critique cannot be that humanity seeks to snuggle down in nature as its environment, but that it seeks to correct in specific ways the consequences of human actions.

T. Koch has formulated basic clarifications of the relationship of "nature" and "subject" in theological terms: "Der Leib und die Natur. Zum christlichen Naturverständnis," NZ, syst. ThRPh 20 (1978): 294ff.

This discussion of the structural elements that are found in the response made by the ethical tradition culminates in the assertion of the meaning that creation has for ethics. The systematic conclusion is that this answer in all its relationships is applicable to humankind as the subjects of ethical thought. It expresses in a variety of ways the "for us" of the givenness of life as an ethical task. The lesson to be drawn from all this is that ethics is not exhausted in this answer and its structure. The indicative dimension of ethics sets the theme for the imperative inherent within it. In this way we can be assured that the relationship of ethics to a subject is based on reality. But the dependence of ethics on a subject is not thereby finally settled. It must be allowed to speak on its own terms. That is the task of the second methodological journey through the basic elements of ethics.

b. The Structure of Ethics in the Answer of the Conduct of One's Own Life

What are the most important points of view that play a role in ethics when we examine the answer of leading one's own life?

The analysis of the answer of the ethical tradition followed the basic thought of the givenness of life in its individual elements. Now the answer of leading one's own life deals with the structural elements that can be developed from the task of giving life. That task can be expressed in this formula: After the question of how the "ought" appears in the "is," we now are to look at the question of how the "is" is contained in the "ought." Leading one's own life is the fulfillment of a position taken in respect to life. Life must be lived, it must be "led." Every ought is addressed to someone. This quite elementary assumption is to be methodically explored and analysed in its various elements for the structure of ethics.

"The real heart and the true meaning of modern ethics is the ethics of the individual" (W. Trillhaas, *Ethik*, 3d ed., 1970, p. 173). And yet modern ethics is only the consistent pursuit of a conception which in the form of the ethic of character has the whole of Western history as its presupposition. It is concerned with the central meaning of the individual human being for the reality of ethics.

The catalogues of virtues and vices in the Apostolic and Post-Apostolic literature show how by taking over ancient lists of virtues the early Christians laid claim to the conduct of the Christian life for the ethical realization of the new faith. In the Pauline writings the catalogues are Rom. 1:29–31; 13:13; 1 Cor. 5:10–11; 6:9–10; 2 Cor. 12:20–21; Gal. 5:19–21; Eph. 4:31; 5:3–4; Col. 3:5, 8; 1 Tim. 1:9–10; 2 Tim. 3:2–5. They find their summation and positive culmination in the triad of "Faith, hope, love" in 1 Cor. 13:13.

We must not underestimate the importance that the living of one's own life has for ethics. On the contrary, it must be brought fully into play in opposition to a tendency that frequently appears in theological thought. Ethics regards the empirical human being as a center of resistance that must be overcome. In this, ethics is following the concept that each one must become another person, must change, reform, be transformed; must turn life around and relearn everything. It all comes down to this, that the reality of ethics is the reality of an actual, empirically formed living of life. Living is the practice, in relation to which all else is to be regarded only as theory. The question that must be asked about method is, how can the "is" of ethics become anchored in the "ought" of living? In the construction of an ethic it is necessary to clarify what fundamental significance the conduct of life has for ethics. Are human beings in their lives merely "recipients" and "appliers" of commands and requirements that are anchored elsewhere? Is it a kind of industry that takes the basic material of ethics produced elsewhere and turns it into finished products? If so, we can ignore people and develop a purely theological ethic untouched by human hands, or regard humans as vexatious trouble makers constrained by an ethic that is closed and complete in itself. On the model of the New Testament theology of "hearers of the word" and of "doers of the word" (James 1:22), recent Protestant theology, under the weight of a topheavy dogmatism, has largely decided to devote its intention to the "hearers of the word." But is not the "hearer of the word" also the one who is responsible for applying what is heard to the reality of life's activities? Is it not intended that what is to be heard should play a role in the life and actions of people? The important thing is that it is in human life that the "ought" finds its reality. The rational character of ethics as the rightness of the way we live is the content that is to be made manifest here. An ethic always implies the living of one's own life.

We can agree with Trillhaas when he says that virtue "is the basis of moral acts" (op. cit., p. 166). The concept of virtue is to be understood as the way in which the "ought" itself comes to constitute a reality that is appropriate to human life and then takes form in the conduct of that life. As the practice of living, "virtue" is a productive category for ethics. It not only gives reality to ethical principles that have been handed down, but it also modifies, forms and renews them in the process of living. And that is exactly what the theoretical concerns of ethics intend.

But more is involved than just the traditional concept of virtue and giving contemporary relevance to the elements of the history of virtue. It is important to bring the theory to bear on defining and specifying the structural elements which can be found for ethics in the idea of leading one's own life.

Our procedure will be to discuss the theme under five headings, which are derived from the five points discussed under the second of the two basic elements of the reality of life — the giving of life.

1) From Principles to Decisions

"Morality regains its living power when ordinary people have learned anew to decide for themselves what principles they should live by" (R. M. Hare, *The Language of Morals*, 1961, p. 73). Hare investigated in detail the question of why it is not adequate to base ethics on general principles, why on the contrary decisions must be made by each person, decisions that then affect the validity and content of principles. It is a matter of self-determination understood in the good sense as the free acknowledgement that one is sharing (op. cit., pp. 45–46) in the ethical task, through which the "external" commandments are productively changed into one's own "inner" obligation. The significance of living in the structure of ethics can first of all be explained by defining the relationship between principles and decisions. This implies a discussion of the theme "autonomy" in relation to the ethical biography of human beings.

If we follow Hare's analysis (op. cit., pp. 81ff.) the line of argument runs as follows. When we learn to do something we are always learning a principle. For example, this is the case when we learn facts. When a pupil is asked to name the tributaries of the Danube, he or she learns to answer, "Iller, Lech, Isar, Inn, to the Danube all flow in." In this case the pupil is also learning the principle of recitation. The learning of an activity is always also the learning of a principle by which the activity is to be carried out. It is never merely the learning of an isolated, individual activity. We learn to carry out activities of a specific sort in a specific sort of situation. But the individual action is not learned in this way. It is a matter of a special decision that must be made independently in relationship to general principles. There is a dynamic relationship between principles and decisions. Thus we do not postulate a realm of pure decisions, free of principles, but the independence of the decisions that are necessary in the process of living is shown in relationship to the principles.

The decisions, however, are not purely situational decisions, that is, the mere application of a principle to a given situation. They are also the expansion or the extension of the principles by which we decide. And they bring about a modification of the principles. A good driver never stops learning. Therefore the principles which we can learn in general are provisional in nature. The decisions we make in living our lives are thus not merely modifications of general principles that are provisional in reference to our individual lives. We are the ones who make these principles binding. They become a genuine "ought" through the living of our own life. This reveals the meaning of the principles in distinction to their general, formal form. In the example of driving a car, the exceptions teach us something. The general rule says to use the turn signal when changing direction. In case a child suddenly runs in front of the car it makes sense to keep both hands on the steering wheel and turn at once without giving a signal. Principles show their meaning for guiding conduct when, as we live our lives, they remain open to the specific individual cases in which the issue is to live and act sensibly.

If we formulate this in more general and abstract terms, we could say that ethical principles have self-determination as their goal. In the leading of our own lives we should realize the autonomy that is immanent in ethics. The tendency of ethics is toward ethical freedom.

Hare applied his reasoning concretely to the problems of education, and in so doing gave us an important reformulation of the ethical dimension of the much discussed topic of socialization.

In the process of education we are dealing with an especially important example of the relationship between principles and the conduct of the individual's life. How should I bring up my children? Surely not to be automatons that simply imitate everything that their elders have done. Education involves the basic principle of flexibility in the way in which we use principles in making moral decisions. Quite sensibly a system of education is not built on the model of an anthill, but in such a way that an important role is played by the way one leads one's own life. Even though the basic rules of ethical living come to us first in the form of external authority, they must become the inner authority by which we live our lives.

The problem can be illustrated by looking at its extremes. The relationship of parents to their children can be perceived in such a way that the children hold strictly to the principles of their parents and make no decisions of their own. That would be possible only if they were confronted exclusively with the same situations their parents faced, that is, if they had no life of their own to lead. Or the relationship of parents to children can be so structured that the parents have no confidence in their own principles. The children then make their own decisions without principles. But it is impossible to start from point zero. In the decisions which the children make other principles are at work, those of their friends or of the world around them. In reality, the children must learn to distinguish and mediate between their own new decisions and principles that are presented to them and that they accept. The relation between generations is thus one of the most significant cases of the living, dynamic relationship between principles and decisions. Thus the history of ethics can be seen as the history of the relation between generations, as the history of constant change and steady continuity. It is vital therefore to learn principles in such a way that they will give us the occasion and the challenge to make decisions on which principles can be based and by which principles are changed, improved, or given new form.

This principle, put in general terms, says ethical principles tend to be made real and reconstructed in the on-going living of life. Living then helps constitute the meaning of the validity of principles. The individual ethical meaning of decisions can be missed through passive dependence on principles as well as by the absence of principles. On this point, Hare said, "If we only teach principles without giving the learner opportunity to incorporate them into his own decisions, that is like teaching natural science exclusively out of textbooks without even entering a laboratory. If on the other hand, we let our child or student driver follow his own self-expression, it is like placing a young man in a laboratory and telling him, 'Do something.' He can have fun or he can kill himself in the process, but he will never learn much about natural science" (op. cit., p. 76).

We can also raise the corresponding question of whether anyone can learn ethics without having experienced life first hand. And it is just as impossible for living to be understood as a pure process of self-discovery.

The process of living is a process in which ethical responsibility is intensified. Its goal is "moral maturity" (Hare), as the reconciliation of principles and decisions. That is essentially a biographical process. Older persons may be inclined to speak only of principles and so to forget the role of their own decisions in the formation of the principles that are binding for them. They need to be advised not to "cramp the child in the adult." Those who are growing up tend to speak about all of their own experiences. It is difficult for them to recognize principles and authorities, even though they follow them one way or another. Thus as a biographical process it moves along a straight line, but it is a process that continues throughout life. We might define the relationship of principles and experiences by saying that principles make individual ethical decisions possible, because not always is everything at stake. They make it possible to concentrate on the reality of one's own life and one's own responsibility. But they remain vital because they are renewed in the process of living one's life. Otherwise they would lose their credibility.

From the relationship of principles and decisions we can also learn something that helps us attain a more precise theological understanding of Christian freedom, and to draw an important consequence that is closely bound up with it. The turning point in the Christian consciousness of freedom as formulated by Paul can be more fully explained in this connection. (I am building here on the discussion above, pp. 47–49). The distinction between the letter of the law and the spirit of the demands of the law brings freedom, because the fulfilling of the law is the discovery of the meaning of the law given in the life and teaching of Jesus Christ. The path from principles to decisions, as a "dynamic relation," contributes to a firmer, more precise, grasp of the nature of this turning point in the structuring of ethics. The turning point is not that a new law has replaced the old law. If the debate over whether there is a new Christian law is pursued in this direction it will lead us astray. Rather, it is the case that through Christian freedom it has become possible for us to take part in our own lives in the living reality of the moral agent who is bound by the law to God's will. By trust in this participation Christian ethics takes on a dynamic meaning that vitalizes the living of life. What is new in the Christian life in relation to the law is found in the living of human life by participating in the inner formation of "principles." In this way, as ethical subjects human beings attain a new status.

This trust involves an important consequence that shows the ethical seriousness of the line of argument developed above in a lighter vein. As the ethical relevance of life is intensified the individual human risk is increased. The way is open to the possibility of human guilt. We can speak of guilt in both an ethical and a theological sense wherever humans are themselves involved in the formation of ethical principles. The concept of guilt is not fully defined as long as we are thinking only of the failure to fulfill outwardly imposed requirements. By contrast, the Christian understanding of guilt is based on the position that human beings are addressed as those who through the conduct of their own lives are involved in building up the binding character of the good. The seriousness of guilt is a result of this dignity, which lets human beings be more than mere receivers of commands, and which lays claim to them as independent and responsible subjects in making the good a reality—that is to say, they are addressed as people of God. Therefore the history of ethics in the Christian world is intimately connected with sensitivity to the reality of guilt. It keeps present before us the ethical and theological weight that Christianity assigns to the leading of one's own life (see also above, pp. 45).

2) From Ethical Decisions to the Formation of a Life Plan

"The wise man's path leads upward to life" (Prov. 15:24). "He who guards his way preserves his life" (Prov. 16:17).

In an old but always new religious metaphor, life is spoken of as a road, a path. One's life is not the sum of individual decisions, but the total form given to a life in an individual manner. The whole of life should find realization as the way of life. Ethical orientation means leading one's life by the formation of a life plan. Under this second point by which we seek to give precise definition to the basic elements of the answer of living one's own life we are concerned with an ethic for a way of life. This is not the path of a lonely wanderer, but a road on which one's life is expanded in relation to life in general, and which therefore faces the question of one's usefulness in the ethical economy of life.

I am following here a line of argument developed by Kurt Beier, which follows the ethical question in a debate with the Anglo-Saxon tradition of utilitarianism (K. Beier, *The Moral Point of View. A Rational Basis of Ethics*, 1958). See also the article by F. Kambartel, "Theo-Logisches," ZEE 15 (1971): 32–35. A good introduction to utilitarianism is N. Hoerster's book *Utilitaristische Ethik und Verallgemeinerung*, 1971. Representative texts with commentary are collected in O. Hoeffe, *Einführung in die utilitaristische Ethik. Klassische und zeitgenössische Texte*, 1975. Here only one aspect of utilitarianism and not the whole of its breadth will be dealt with.

The common opinion that there is a conflict between utility and morality is a prejudice that cannot be maintained for any correct discussion of ethics. (See the discussion of the relationship between duty and happiness, above, pp. 71, 113.) On the contrary, a discussion of the question of utility helps to attain a richer concept of the way we lead our lives in relation to the lives of others.

A useful line of argument seeks to show why the formation of an ethically oriented life plan better ensures the achieving of utility as maximizing success in life than does the pursuit of immediate personal interests. The method to be followed is to ask the question of the bases for action. What are good, intelligible bases for our actions? This question plays a role in deciding whether in specific cases we should rely on immediate advantage or stand on a moral position. Let us assume a case in which we must decide to lie or tell the truth. If one lies, we must ask why. What reasons can be given for doing so? The answer might be that it was useful to lie. If I had told the truth I would have found myself in a difficult situation. That can count as a good, that is, intelligible reason. It makes that action plausible.

When on the other hand in a corresponding situation one does not lie and as a result really does get into trouble, we can again ask why. What reason can be given for doing so? The answer might be that I told the truth even though it got me into trouble. But in future situations I can count on being regarded as reliable. That is more important to me than the temporary advantage I might have gained by lying. That too can be regarded as a good, intelligible reason. Here as well the action is based on my interests, in this case a long term interest that takes into account the short term disadvantages. In addition this answer has the advantage of being in harmony with the moral rule, thou shalt not lie. This means that an action and the reason for it can be openly acknowledged at the same time and in the same place. In the case of a lie that is not possible. The fact that the person told a lie must be concealed. The usefulness of the act is thus dependent on the calculation that the lie will not be discovered. But this makes the success of the act dependent on circumstances over which the one acting has no control "Lies have short legs." Even without drawing out the casuistry of this case any further it is easy to see the general implications. They can be established by a comparison of the reasons, by asking which are the better reasons.

There are two further lines of argument that bear on the formation of a life plan. Those reasons must be regarded as better which allow me to act in a manner conducive to my well-being over the long run. In the long run the moral reasons are better, because they are able to protect the identity and stability of my life's course in widely differing and changing situations. If on the other hand I pursue non-moral reasons which lead me to lie or steal, to be untrue or deceitful, then perhaps I can count on a short term advantage or gain, but I cannot expect that this will lead to long term advantage or to a life that is meaningful to me as an individual. In fact such an outcome is highly unlikely. The better reasons are thus those that serve all aspects of my life. It is intelligible to decide for the moral bases of action. The whole of life is a more important goal than momentary success.

A second line of argument may be added to this. The better grounds are those that make it possible for me to live my life together with other persons. By their structure, moral reasons work toward the coexistence of differing life plans. That is their purpose. An individual may appear to be at a disadvantage in reference to his or her life goals because of taking account of the life plan of others. But because no one can live entirely alone, and because the pursuit of one's own life plan without consideration of the plans of others is possible only to the detriment of others, it is better to take those plans into account. This makes the chances better that over the long run everyone may achieve greater well-being. The compatibility of life plans, the possibility of their existing together has for this reason a higher degree of moral reasonableness. It is better to rely on moral reasons than to pursue an unmodified egoism.

The good reasons for acting in such a manner can be brought together in a rule as follows: Act in such a manner that each action is taken in relation to a life plan. The extension of the rule would be: Form your life plan in such a manner that your own life will be compatible with that of others. Ethical consistency in life is better than a life oriented to immediate advantage. Basically we have reconstructed the content of what earlier ethical theory meant when it explained virtue in terms of a virtuous life. The concept of virtue has fallen into disrepute, especially because of its casuistic division into individual virtues. It is not important to try to restore the concept to a place of honor. What is important is to ensure that life not be determined by the individual, specific actions that make it up, but by the whole way it is lived under the guidance of ethical principles. This is the contribution which the conduct of an individual life can bring in a productive way to the construction of a general ethic.

The formation of a life plan through the leading of one's own life contributes much to the topic of the correspondence of individual and general public ethics. Any one who wants to participate in the public discussion of ethical standards, for example in the social ethical themes of politics and society that are in the foreground today, must also be willing to listen to what is said about the structuring of his or her own individual life.

This is probably the insight that led E. Wolf to postulate the renewal of the concept of virtue in the realm of political virtue (E. Wolf, "Grundlinien einer evangelischen Tugendlehre des Politischen," in the collection he edited, *Sozialethik. Theologische Grundfragen*, 1975, pp. 332ff.).

Justice is then the principle of an equalization of differing life plans, in the achieving of which the reality of the life of others is included in the structure of one's own conduct of life and plays a role there. Justice is therefore more than a mere ideal; it is more realistic than egoism.

J. Rawls has developed a large-scale theory of justice that seeks to develop this point of view in detail. It is concerned especially with the political and economic composition of the world. This theory will be discussed later in the concrete issues of ethics (John Rawls, *Theory of Justice*, 1972).

If the reader has followed the discussion to this point, then the reasons why each individual should adopt a moral standpoint in the conduct of each life will be plausible. This detailed discussion of ethics in an individual's life is not intended to promote "individualism." In the formation of a life plan one's own life is brought into relation with life "in general" and thus becomes a life for and with others. The "ought" that is based in the distinctive nature of the individual life includes the obligation which as the social aspect of one's life is determined from within. The structure of that obligation will be the theme of the next point in our analysis.

3) From Social Roles to Personal Responsibility

"There has arisen a world of attributes without a man, of experiences without anyone who experiences them, and it seems almost as if in the ideal case no human being would ever again experience anything privately, and the friendly burden of personal responsibility would dissolve in a system of formulas of various possible meanings. It is possible that the final dissolution of the anthropocentric attitude, which for so long a time has held that humanity is the center of the universe, but which now for centuries has been decreasing, has finally arrived at the ego itself" (Robert Musil, *Der Mann ohne Eigenschaften*, 1931, 1970, p. 150).

Sociologically trained readers regard Musil as having anticipated in his great novel the modern theory of roles. The role is the smallest social unit that sociology can identify. Behind it begins immediately the sociological no man's land of human individuality and personality. A role defines functions in a social system, and these functions are life in social terms. But does this not mean that when I take on a role I do not do what I want to do, but what others, want, ultimately what society wants of me? Isn't the formula "trust is the inner meaning of sociality" (see above, pp. 55–57) merely a euphemism, against which resistance must be aroused, resistance which is expressed in that protest slogan "alienation"?

Following the method of this investigation of the structural elements of ethics, we must stress that one's own life is through and through social reality, in that it is always lived under the expectations which others have of us. To lead one's own life means then to lead it for others, a situation that is always the case, quite apart from any position that we ourselves take.

Ethics always implies a life for others. The role theory presents elements which describe the structure of this social form of life in a manner from which there is no appeal. The question of why I should do something thus finds an obvious and relatively undramatic answer.

R. Dahrendorf introduced into German thought the sociological theory of roles on the basis of the emigration to America, and worked out in detail its continental-European presuppositions (R. Dahrendorf, *Homo sociologicus. Ein Versuch zur Geschichte, Bedeutung und Kritik der sozialen Rolle*, 1959, 9th ed., 1970).

On the strength of that movement the theory of the "expectation of expectation" of G. H. Mead received wider acceptance (G. H. Mead, *Mind, Self and Society*, 1934). The problem in fundamental philosophy of the relation of subject and society, which constitutes the background of the theory of society, need not be gone into here. H. Schelsky had the insight that sociology is not able to acknowledge the human subject as such in the living of human life. He expressed it in the concept of a merely "negative sociology," that is, a sociological theory that explicitly defines its boundaries to exclude the free subject who acts (*Ortsbestimmung der Soziologie*, 1959, pp. 93ff.). He recognized the question of the role of the subject in society as a key question for the theory of society (for example in his study, *Der Mensch in der wissenschaftlich-technischen Zivilization*, 1961, reprinted in *Auf der Suche nach Wirklichkeit*, 1965, pp. 439–80). J. Habermas, in spite of otherwise very different epistemological interests, greeted Schelsky as an ally against functionalistic system theory, because this theory can dispense with the individual subject altogether. J. Habermas, *Legitimationsprobleme im Spätkapitalismus*, 1973, pp. 192ff., in debate with the work of N. Luhmann; on this debate see T. Rendtorff, *Gesellschaft ohne Religion?*, 1976, esp. pp. 25ff.; cf. the book by J. Habermas and N. Luhmann, *Theorie der Gesellschaft oder*

Sozialtechnologie, 1971; Th. W. Adorno, out of the problematic relation of subject and society, developed the basic perspective for his major work, *Negative Dialektik*, 1966.

Role theory is basically concerned with such phenomena as the following: The conduct of an individual's life is conditioned throughout by the fact that we are here for others "as" someone, "as" father or son, "as" mother or daughter, "as" teacher or pupil, "as" member of parliament or taxpayer, "as" worker or entrepreneur, and so forth. We are that which we are for others, not simply as a person, but in the specific manner of roles that define the expectations which others have of us. Roles are assumed therefore, and the construction of a specific way of life is carried out through assuming roles. They constitute our social identity. They integrate our own life into the social fabric of life with others and for others. We must begin by picturing to ourselves the undramatic, but relevant situation of which we become conscious in a new, sociological manner.

The matter is not new at all. The category of role in sociology and social ethics means the same thing as the old concept of rank with its ethical view of office and profession. The Lutheran doctrine of the two realms, so disputed today, functioned as a scheme for ordering social ranks. G. Müller is thus on firm ground when he says that this involves a sort of "social description," that is, a descriptive sociology that at the same time formulates ethical norms. See G. Müller in N. Hasselmann, ed., *Gottes Wirken in seiner Welt. Zur Diskussion um die Zwei-Reiche-Lehre*, vol. 1, 1980.

The role defines the ethical responsibility of being and living "as one" to be the duty to lead one's life in a manner appropriate to one's status. The Lutheran doctrine of calling undermined the hierarchical nature of the traditional doctrine of ranks. Every calling and every status defines the "role" of a human being "as" one who is to live for others, independent of the position of this role in the social hierarchy of values. The proverbial maid who sweeps the threshing floor stands on the same level with the ruling prince. This was progress toward a structural view of role that points to the modern period. In addition, Luther brought new ethical intensity to the doctrine of roles by interpreting its ethical obligation theologically as God's call, regardless of social distinctions. This is closely connected with Luther's teaching that there is a fundamental difference between a person's reputation before God, and that person's reputation before the world. If a person's reputation in the eyes of God is independent of social position, thanks to the doctrine of justification, then social roles are freed from the burden of being bearers of the ultimately valid relationship to God by faith, that is, the burden of defining one's own "inner" identity. Roles are relegated to their appropriate worldly status, and are seen in terms of their function.

It is now possible to state more precisely the issue involved here. If a social role is defined by the expectations that others have of the one in that role, then to take on a role means to take on the expectations which others have of us. As a rule, however, they are not expectations of the "person," as defined in that person's own self-understanding, but expectations of the accomplishments which the person can perform for others because of that role. No one expects a sales clerk to reveal her inner life or to provide pastoral comfort. The bus driver is expected to drive the prescribed route, but not to make suggestions about the proper way to life or the goal of those riding the bus. And so forth.

A role is "mastered" when it is taken on independently, that is, when the expectations of others are anticipated by the one playing the role. For this situation Mead used the formula, "expectation of expectations," that is the role player by his or her own expectation anticipates the expectation which others have because of the role. In contrast to the theoretical model of the equality in rank of the subjects developed in the theory of community of communication, the role-specific differences are quite important for role theory. The "for" others takes on the specific form of "as" one who is in a specific role. This includes and makes specific the meaning of "for" others.

Roles are an extension of one's own way of living and of the possibilities of an individual life. By means of roles each person participates in contexts that go beyond a purely individual competence. The office holder not only has different powers from those of a private person, but clearly has more power. Without going into the possible dangers of misuse of power which are important in moral discourse, this point of view needs to be stressed. By means of social roles something new enters the lives of men and women — tasks and responsibilities, not unreasonable demands, but an expansion of life. By the conferring of roles something is added to human life that does not come from the individual's own self. Roles give the individual life a greater share of "reality." This is the moral basis which justifies the expectations, that is, the actions that are expected from and demanded of the one who plays the role.

This is also why the role is not exhausted by the meaning the role player ascribes to it, either in biographical terms or by interpretation. Roles have a relative social objectivity in relation to their subjective self-definition. For this reason they are highly significant for communication between subjects. We can and must reach understanding on the function of specific roles, independently of any differences of philosophical outlook, faith, or convictions. Roles are an important link in the chain of social responsibility and social trust. Even if we are not aware of this we notice it when someone steps out of the role and does not do what is normally expected. Other persons have good reasons for not understanding what is happening.

M. Honecker made use of role theory in combination with a suggestion for a new way of explaining the world in terms of the distinction between the two ways God rules the world in the context of the Lutheran doctrine of two realms (M. Honecker, *Sozialethik zwischen Tradition und Vernunft*, 1977, pp. 229ff.).

If we ask what consequences such a phenomenology of social roles has for the ethical structure of our own lives, we must consider one more fact of the picture. The individual is not confined to a single role, but lives at the intersection of various roles. Therefore neither as singular nor plural is the social role a complete definition of our way of life. That would be an inadmissible overextension of the concept. Roles do not define a closed world of activities, but the openness of our own life for the social context. The practical challenge for the way we live which is contained in the role is that each of us must strive to achieve our individual integration of differing, even heterogeneous roles. This brings us to the theme of conflict of roles. Such conflicts can arise in which at one and the same time differing roles, which may even get in each other's way, must be acknowledged: The father of a family who is also expected to be a good son to his elderly parents, an active church member, an alert and politically aware citizen, and in his profession a capable worker, to mention only a few examples, must lead his life under the pressure of conflicting roles. The individual will find that the plurality of roles is just as problematic as the individual role is obvious and free of problems. This shows that roles do not put an end to the independence of an individual's life, but that they lay claim to and even demand such independence.

The end of the "ego," of which the Musil quotation spoke, was proclaimed prematurely. The individual's consciousness arises out of that multiplicity of roles. Success in reconciling the conflicts can lead to an intensification of moral self-awareness, and ability in dealing with various roles will be experienced as an increase in the ability to lead one's own life. But it is also possible for the drama of the conflict to be overwhelming. Then the ethical reflection on our way of living that is implicit in the social roles finds explicit expression. The question is: Can I really maintain my own standpoint? Is it through my role that I am everything that I am, and who am I really apart from my role? This is another form of the question which was posed in the preceding section: Should I attempt to take a moral standpoint at all? Is the whole role theory only the description of a drama on the stage, and after the performance the actress sets the role aside in order to be "herself" again? And when or where would it be possible for her to be exclusively "herself"?

For Protestant ethics this is the place to consider Luther's distinction between "Christ person" and "world person," because it deals with the conflict we have been considering. As "world person" the individual is viewed in terms of functions for others. This is not an optional role that could be dropped if we so desired. The role could be dropped only by refusing to be a human being in a specific, individual, and responsible way, by attempting to be "human in general." This would be to give up one's own role, to negate self. For such a negation another position is needed. As "Christ person" one is indeed understood in contrast to a "world person." As "Christ person" one enters into the role which God gives to the one who is accepted and set free, the role which God has designed for that individual. Even here individuals are not "themselves" in an abstract and immediate sense, but they are what they are through what God is for them. Putting this theological idea into the language of role theory, it means that the "for others" and the "as one" of the roles are reversed and applied to the "self" of the human individual. The power with which an individual life enters into the service of others, the commitment of one's own life, has as its precedent a life "for us," that is, God's accessibility to humanity. The term "Christ person" expresses that we "ourselves," independent of the "world person" and its social roles, can be that which God is "for us." That God "in Christ" took on the role of a human being is an action that could be understood as an interpretation of Christology in terms of role theory. If we reflect further, it becomes clear that what a person is as a "world person" in social roles for others, that person cannot be for himself or herself. But since the social roles, as is shown by the conflict of roles, imply an independent conduct of one's life, we must become conscious of the independence of our own life in relation to them. Thus in the structure of ethics the question moves us beyond the concept of roles to the question of our conduct of our own life as the place where freedom is to be found.

On the distinction between "Christ person" and "world person" in Luther's thought, F. Lau's work, *"Äusserliche Ordnung" und "Weltlich Ding"* in *Luther's Theologie,* 1933, is informative. Extensive discussions are also found in P. Althaus, *The Ethics of Martin Luther,* 1972 and F. Gogarten, *Luthers Theologie,* 1967.

E Jüngel explored in detail the difference between "inner" and "outer" person, the question of freedom in his *Zur Freiheit eines Christenmenschen. Eine Erinnerung an Luthers Schrift,* 1978.

One further question remains to be dealt with here. Is there not also a conflict between mutually exclusive roles? And isn't the distinction "world person" and "Christ person" an exemplary case of such a conflict of roles? It has been a widely accepted practice to deal with this question in terms of whether the "Christian" does not have to play a role that is totally different from that of the "worldly" role player.

The question can take on quite different forms. Can someone say that as a Christian I may not take part in the persecution of Jews, but in my role as a public official I must do so in certain cases? This is clearly a false phrasing of the issue. Even the role of public official forbids taking part in the persecution of Jews. The unreasonable demand to persecute Jews represents a conflict in the role of the official itself, because there are no valid reasons for such persecution. The role defines only one element in the structure of ethics. It is the concrete place at which such questions as those we have already examined become relevant. Neither from the point of view of a life plan nor of a decision on the basis of principles can there be in such a case an adequate basis for the "worldly" action in response to such a demand. The same would be true if we applied the criteria that are contained in the answer of the ethical tradition — the construction of a world, the formation of tradition, and so forth. The question can also be phrased: Isn't the Christian always obliged to play another, quite different role? But it would be thoroughly false to assume that the Christian occupies a special position which provides an escape from the conflict of roles, or puts the Christian in the pleasant situation of being above such conflict and thus creates the impression that everyone else is of lesser moral worth. The reality of the conflict of roles cannot be covered over by a stereotyped religious verdict. An attitude of moral superiority always arises when someone is not dealing with actual problems or does not accept concretely defined responsibility.

But "being Christian" plays a role in our "being human," indeed a very decisive role. No one who claims to be Christian has any reason for declining to accept roles assigned by society, but will acknowledge and accept them. Such a person knows, however, that the leading of one's own life does not free one from an independent maintenance of those roles. In an empirical case of conflict we will therefore take on ourselves the consequences of opposition by bearing empirical suffering. A consciousness of being free is impossible without this individual courage. Indeed even the exceptional situation of extreme conflict is a circumstance that calls for confirmation *in* the world.

It also follows from this that it is necessary to keep the world of roles open, to demand the establishment of a world in which the various roles can be harmonized with one another. In this the empirical existence of the church plays a sociologically definable role by playing an independent role. A world that does not acknowledge the empirical independence of the church is not organized sensibly. The reference to the "inner" freedom of Christians becomes a farce wherever the church is unable to function independently in society.

4) Freedom as an Unconditional Yes to One's Own Life: Conscience

"Do that which makes you worthy to be happy" (Kant, *Kritik der reinen Vernunft*, PhB. 37 a, B 836f. [*Critique of Pure Reason*, 1929]).

Neither the ethical cleverness of a life plan nor the social roles that impose duties on us are end stations of ethical reflection. On the contrary, they are factors that renew reflection. In a further step in the construction of ethics we now inquire into what the empirical place of freedom is in the leading of one's own life. If there is no environment in which we can take refuge as a final home on earth, then it must be possible to assure ourselves of a place in our own lives where we can have that independence which encompasses and supports all obligations and duties.

This is the question of a concept of autonomy that can have meaning for the individual. Here we can learn from Kant.

In this instance too our attempts must be modest. It is not possible to attempt a comprehensive evaluation of Kant's ethical philosophy or of the history of its study and interpretation. Only one idea will be explored, but one that can make a significant contribution to the course of our presentation. In this we will follow a point of view developed by H. Lübbe in the interpretation of Kant (H. Lübbe, "Dezisionismus in der Moraltheorie

Kants," *Epirrhosis, Festgabe für Carl Schmitt,* 1968, pp. 567ff.). It involves
a commentary on the maxim given at the beginning of this section.

We know of no sure rule by which doing what is good is certain
to be followed by success. On the contrary we have the experience
that we are not in control of the empirical conditions which could
guarantee the achievement of happiness or well-being. When we look
at ourselves we see that our own inclinations and wishes are variable
and changing. One time they are satisfied, and another they are not.
Their content and the value we get from experiencing them are
changeable. Not even when we consider ourselves in the immediate
realm of our sensory experience do we have adequate and comprehensive clarity about what is "good" for us.

In respect to ethics then, what can autonomy mean? This question
must be explored in detail if freedom is to be a meaningful category
for the individual. In any case autonomy cannot mean control of the
totality of conditions under which happiness and success will be ours.
Autonomy does not mean control of external circumstances. Contrary to a widely held understanding, ethical autonomy in Kantian
terms is not a total authority exercised by a self-sufficient human
being who is able to take control of everything. This caricature of
"bourgeois" autonomy which has become popular in Marxist cri-
tiques, and also in theological criticism of the Enlightenment, applies
only to decadent forms of autonomy and does not recognize the ethical seriousness of the concept of autonomy.

The problem of autonomy as a concept for freedom arises out of
the actual experience of unfreedom. Autonomy can be taken as a
theme when we deal with the experience we have in simply attaining
well-being in the world. Suffering in the world, the unyielding nature
of institutional limitations, or of all sorts of natural occurrences, war,
oppressive government, and so forth—all that and much more poses
the problem of freedom as the question of the conditions under which
autonomy is possible. But even in the relationship to one's own self,
there arises the problem of autonomy as freedom in relationship to
one's own hopes for happiness. Because happiness is not subject to our
calculations, is easily lost, is soon past, especially when we think that
we have it, it provides no permanent freedom. No one who relies on
happiness alone is autonomous.

If we are to talk of autonomy, we must talk of a concept of freedom
that is significant for the individual. It must be related to conditions

over which we can exert control, and in the control of which we are autonomous — freedom as the reality of one's own freedom.

"Do that which makes you worthy to be happy." Kant developed a line of argument according to which the only means at our disposal for attaining to the "highest good" is that we show ourselves worthy of it. Empirical ideas of happiness, wishes, hopes, do not constitute freedom. It can only be contained in such a rule as can actually be followed in the conduct of our own life. This rule then is not conditional because it formulates one sole condition, the fulfillment of which depends on us ourselves, and therefore that which it promises, that is, to be worthy of happiness, can be deemed attainable insofar as this fulfillment lies within our own power. They are free who insist only on that which is within their own power. Thus Kant formed an emphatic concept of freedom as unconditioned autonomy, because its conditions are not subject to the will of another but only to our own will. And he constructed this concept in such a manner that it coincides with the ethical fullness of human life.

It has been objected that Kant's rule for freedom does not take into account concrete legal and moral relationships.

This objection expresses the force of the criticism which Hegel directed against Kant in the development of his ethics (cf. G. W. F. Hegel, *Philosophie des Rechts*, Section 135.).

This objection hits the mark, but it needs to be stated with more precision. Kant includes in the concept of autonomy for living our life that which in reference to the human world we have called an unconditional yes to reality (see above, p. 114). The Kantian rule of freedom as autonomy can be valid under quite varied legal and moral relationships. It is not restricted to any specific system of property or specific form of family structure. It sets up an obligatory rule by which first and foremost the identity of the free subject is established. To this extent the rule agrees with the general structure of the Kantian maxim: Act in such a manner that your intention could be everyone's intention. The categorical imperative in all its versions is not a contribution to a concrete duty ethic, but to a duty ethic on the basis of freedom.

For various versions of the categorical imperative, see Kant's *Grundlegung der Metaphysik der Sitten, Werke*, ed. Weischedel, IV, p. 43; *Kritik der praktischen Vernunft*, ibid., p. 140, etc. Kant's contemporaries found instruction for concrete virtues and duties much more readily in the book of Freiherr von Knigge, who presented to the rising middle class in detail the moral reasoning that made up a respectable life. But this, like all guides to conduct, fell victim to the historical law of going out of date (Adolph Freiherr von Knigge, *Über den Umgang mit Menschen*, 1788, 3d ed. 1790; new edition by G. Meding, 1977, [Insel Pocketbook 273]).

The question, What should we do? has been carried back to the theory of what contribution is unconditionally at our disposal to make toward the realization of a moral world: The will to act according to our best knowledge and conscience, only with the intention that our actions have universal validity, that is, to show oneself as worthy of general happiness. This morality is autonomous in that the duty to which it binds us is independent of the external conditions under which we live. By acting morally, people make themselves free. This involves also a renunciation, a renunciation of the thought that one could grasp the whole world, its natural and historical, moral and social conditions, in order to make it into a good world. In this respect Kant was extremely skeptical. But he was not a skeptic about the conditions that make autonomy possible in respect to ethics. On the contrary. Anyone who soberly considers the real conditions under which we live has no reason to deny freedom. Rather we are stimulated to identify freedom wherever it can be perceived as "unconditioned." For the sum of the matter is: Whatever you do according to this rule is right in any case, regardless of whether it succeeds or not. Those are autonomous who submit only to this rule of freedom.

Being independent of success does not mean that autonomous ethical actions allow us to regard the outcome as a matter of indifference (cf. the discussion above, pp. 112–13).

If we adopt Kant's line of argument for our structuring of ethics, the result may be stated thus: An ethic always implies an unconditional yes to one's own life. Whatever the empirical circumstances under which we live our life, we can live as independent and responsible agents only in a framework of personal responsibility, in the consciousness that it is our own life we are living. Only by our acceptance of life can this life become a contribution to the universal good.

This freedom can also be discussed in relation to its inner social nature. Because it is ethically defined freedom, it cannot be the abstract freedom of an isolated individual. The life of others also plays a role in our freedom, because a contribution to the general realization of the good always implies giving life to others. The place where "others" are involved in the consciousness of our freedom is our conscience.

Ethically determined freedom does not involve self-glorification, pure self-determination, or self-discovery. Autonomy cannot be defined in ethical terms as self-sufficiency. To use the now familiar expressions of this present study, the key is how the givenness of life and the giving of life are basically connected with each other and how it is shown in the living of our life that they belong together unconditionally. The place where this occurs is our conscience. In the course of the construction of ethics we now come to the reasons why the concept of conscience is introduced at this point and what problems are thereby clarified.

First, a few references to the doctrine of conscience should be given. "Reflection on conscience belongs in the center of the doctrine of the person who acts" (W. Trillhaas, *Ethik*, 3d ed., 1970, p. 11; there also are found further references to the literature, e.g., pp. 100–112, "Ausführungen zum Gewissensbegriff." See also the article on conscience by H. Reiner in *Historisches Wörterbuch der Philosophie*, vol. 3, pp. 574–91).

In the doctrine of conscience, three aspects can be clearly seen. First, conscience is included under the natural morality which belongs to each human being. In the Christian tradition the major source of this understanding of conscience is Rom. 2:14–15. Here conscience is described as that faculty which even where the law has not been given one is able to understand the meaning of the law as God's will, because it is "written on the heart." From this are derived arguments for a "natural" morality that is operative in the experience of conscience and in the judgment rendered by conscience.

This argument is especially used in Catholic moral theology. On this point see Th. Müncker, *Die psychologischen Grundlagen der katholischen Sittenlehre*, 1934, 4th ed., 1953. The newer developments in Catholic moral theology are summarized by J. G. Ziegler, *Vom Gesetz zum Gewissen*, 1968. In the most recent development of Catholic moral theology the concept of conscience has become less important than that of Christian freedom, e.g., F. Böckle, *Fundamentalmoral*, 1977 [*Fundamental Concepts of Moral Theology*, 1968]. For the understanding of conscience in the Reformation, see E. Wolf, "Vom Problem des Gewissens in reformatorischer Sicht," *Peregrinatio*, 1954, 2d ed., 1962, pp. 81ff. G. Ebeling adopted Reformation points of view in his own systematic presentation, "Theologische Erwägungen über das Gewissen," *Wort und Glaube* 1, pp. 429–46.

If conscience is regarded as the place where God's will is experienced, this can be understood as meaning that the conscience is also the place where what is normative in general is received, above all, upbringing and the transmission of culture. It testifies to the presence of norms that are born in human beings by nature or are implanted in them. Understood in this way, conscience functions in communicating the same norms as are communicated in social norms or the norms of positive law. The task of conscience is to strengthen and support these general norms from within. In this way the idea of conscience takes on a strongly judicial character. It represents the contents of law and morality before they formulated or codified. Then conscience plays an important role in the possibility of universalizing law, since the moral content of laws is not limited to their codified forms. For the same reason conscience can be the seat of conflict, if there is a growing awareness that social norms which are specifically enforced, systematically codified, or historically accepted may after all be incompatible with universal morality. The independence of conscience reestablishes the distinction between codified moral norms and their general meaning and content. Therefore the concept of conscience is accompanied by the demand for freedom of conscience.

Second, the concept of conscience can establish human independence in relation to God in contrast to our relationship to other persons. Paul frequently used the concept in this sense when speaking of the question of the justification of his apostolic office and the way he fulfilled his office in the face of various attacks (2 Cor. 1:12; Rom. 9:1). And the concept of conscience takes on a new aspect for ethics through being connected with Christian freedom in that Paul teaches that one's own freedom should not be insisted on to the detriment of the conscience of others. This is the idea that one's own — in this case "good"— conscience is limited by the conscience of others. In 1 Cor. 10:23-24 Paul makes a distinction between freedom and the influence of our conduct on others. The concrete case, eating meat sold in the general market that had been sacrificed to idols, is not settled by an explanation of heathen temple rites, but by the exhortation to be considerate of the scruples of the conscience of others. It is a matter of taking their conscience into account, for one's own freedom should not be limited by the conscience of other persons (v. 29). Here the judgment of conscience is unequivocally referred to the way an individual's life is lived. This brings to expression what might be called an inward social nature of conscience.

In the writings of Luther, through whose Bible translation the word "conscience" entered the German vernacular language, we find mention of both the predominantly "bad" conscience and also of the "good" conscience as a joyous and undiscouraged conscience. But in the foreground of the meaning of the concept there is always a different emphasis. For Luther, following tradition, the "bad" human conscience is always that which calls attention to the evil deeds and intentions of sinful human beings. It also points individuals to the demands of God's will. The "joyous" conscience, on the other hand, is the result of Christian liberty, grounded, not in what one is or what one can do, but in a belief in justification, which means liberation from sin and guilt.

In the present day probably the most thorough-going philosophical analysis of conscience is that worked out by Martin Heidegger in *Sein und Zeit* (1927), 7th ed., 1953, pp. 267ff.

The concept of conscience requires that we show how it is related to the unity of the person. To what extent can we say that the "giving of life" for others is necessary for one's own life? Responsible freedom in contrast to self-glorification implies love and forgiveness, but not altruism, because "others" are necessary for our own life.

Here too we will begin with elementary observations. Conscience announces its presence when we do something, intend to do or have done something that is not right or good, and which involves deeds or actions that concern others. Here we have cases in which we say that we have a guilty conscience toward someone. In such cases conscience functions as the continuing consciousness that accompanies our deeds, intentions, and accomplishments. A difference has also been drawn between *prior* pangs of conscience and subsequent pangs. But this difference is secondary in nature. It expresses the experience that conscience is involved in one's course of life as a continuing awareness and is not limited to a completed action or to a verdict on a specific action. This can also bring to expression the fact that conceptions of possible acts, their effects, and their consequences, play a role in addition to that to be considered in the evaluation of an action. Conscience involves that dimension of action which is united with the totality of one's conduct of life, while a judicial verdict on an action is primarily based on a judgment of an individual act.

As a continuing awareness, conscience functions as a relatively independent consciousness in relation to the intentions and actions of human agents. It is the application to our own lives of the effects of possible or actual actions. In conscience we encounter the question of the unity of the person in the light of that person's life as an active life that is made concrete with others and for others. For example, the question of conscience can be formulated as whether I can desire to be really identified with this intention or this action, so that I can say: Yes, that is what I am and what I want to be. Conscience often involves the revealing or disclosing of a self-contradiction. If we concentrate on this aspect, we see it means that in our conscience and through our conscience there is ascribed to the individual person that which as a concrete act or deed carried out has an effect on and influences others. Conscience as the place where the question of the unity of the person is posed contains the challenge of identifying oneself with one's own actions, of recognizing oneself in them, with a yes or no. This extends from feelings that are unpleasant all the way to doubts and bitter self-reproaches. In conscience we become aware of a negation of individual identity, not by a question from outside ourselves, but through ourselves. Thus conscience sets forth the theme of the unity of the individual under the conditions of self-contradiction. But this unity is not thereby lost; it asserts itself as conscience, as the appeal of conscience. In the voice of conscience we hear the demand to hold fast and renew respect for oneself as respect for this unity in the face of the differences in the ways people lead their lives. If a person's conscience is sensitive it is not sensitive to this or that action for which the person is answerable to others, to courts of law, neighbors, fellow humans. No, if one's conscience is sensitive it is sensitive in the unity of the person. This unity brings the unconditioned nature of one's own life into play, even where there is inner contradiction or negation of one's identity, and therefore makes the individual aware that this unity encompasses one's own life as life that has been given to us as well as life that is lived for others. In this sense conscience performs an ethically relevant function for our lives.

In expanding the concept of conscience and defining it more precisely, we can say that in terms of conscience intentions and actions that affect others take on thematic importance, but we can also say that they do not affect one's own life but rather involve the giving of life and the life that is lived for others. By means of conscience we come to know that this life for others is finally necessary for our own life, that it has meaning that involves and helps determine our own life. This situation is expressed in the telling expression that someone can't sleep well because of having done or failed to do, having planned or neglected something or other that affects another person. This expression, which is more than mere metaphor, points also to the connection between the conduct of our ethical life and our physical condition, as for example, in the expression that something has caused a person's hair to turn gray. All these observations lead to the conclusion that actions in respect to others are a necessity in each person's life. This becomes clear in the question of conscience as to whether this or that is something we can live with or not. Conscience is therefore the theme of an ethically guided life that goes beyond separate, empirically defined actions and thus affects not only that which is empirically at our disposal, but also our whole conduct of life as a life lived in responsible freedom. This is the content of the theological idea that conscience addresses humans in their relationship to God.

This points us also to the ethically relevant side of the problem of freedom of conscience. We have already said that the problem of freedom of conscience arises when in specific instances a conflict develops between a "natural" ethical judgment, that is, one lacking official, public status, and clearly defined ordinances or rules of social morality. But that is not a conflict between two equal forces. In a conflict of the individual conscience with a valid law or with the dominant morality it becomes evident that a judgment of conscience, if it prevails, does not have the status of a general legal norm or a prescription that is generally valid for conduct. The valid basis on which it rests is the importance which freedom of belief has in historical perspective for freedom of conscience.

See M. S. Bates, *Religious Liberty*, 1945. On the wider problems involved in freedom of belief, see W. Geiger, "Das Grundrecht der Gewissensfreiheit," in K. Forster, ed., *Staat und Gewissensfreiheit*, 1959.

Indeed the question so widely discussed today of conscientious objection to military service shows clearly that the discussion does not involve legal issues of equal rank. The strength of the right to refuse military service stands and falls by its basis in an individual position, involving responsibility for one's own life, and the freedom of the person loses its meaning when it is recognized as a generally valid alternative. Without wishing to go into the difficult problems involved in dealing pragmatically with the issues involved, it can be said that the basic right to refuse military service for reasons of conscience depends on taking conscience seriously and not letting it degenerate into merely subjective intentions filled out by whatever reasons are convenient.

Freedom of conscience in opposition to state and church has a sound basis for insisting that no one can be forced against his or her conscience to express a conviction or take an action which is generally held or required. This protection of the conscience guarantees the right to live according to the dictates of conscience. But it does not accord to the verdict of the individual conscience the same general normative status as the rule over which the conflict arose. Against this background the advocacy of freedom of conscience also expresses a general claim, that is, a claim that public ordinances be established. The point of this advocacy is not to render judgments of conscience everywhere possible. That would be an outspokenly cynical position, which in the interests of giving vitality to conscience was trying to generate as many conflicts as possible. Rather the opposite position must be stated. The general nature of the advocacy of freedom of conscience leads to seeking to bring about situations in which the public social and political context would give rise as seldom as possible to decisions of conscience. A community should not be constituted in such a manner that its citizens are frequently provoked to assert their freedom of conscience. This would necessarily be regarded as the hallmark of a totalitarian regime, in which decisions of conscience are too frequently, or even permanently required. On the other hand it is characteristic of a liberal community that in it social and political institutions maintain normal conditions and allow wide latitude in practices, so that the decisions of conscience required of its citizens are as few as possible. Political and social situations that cause conflicts of conscience in public life also cause problems of identity. But the sphere of public life is not adapted to providing ultimate human identity in the sense of the unity of the person. The general recognition which freedom of conscience has won in the political and social institutions of the community is much more closely connected with the fact that individual ethical identity has little power over the major organizational forms of state and society. This is a consequence of the emergence of a consciousness of freedom. But we must also realize that the price of individual freedom is a lack of clarity at the political-societal level. That this can result in uncertainty about one's identity and an increase of new problems of identity, shows us once again that "others" are necessary as we lead our own lives. Conscience, when it is clearly defined in its own freedom, is the organ through which the inward social nature of one's own life is expressed.

5) *The Christian Life as the Living Out of Freedom*

"I appeal to you therefore, brethren, by the mercies of God, to present your bodies as a living sacrifice, holy and acceptable to God, which is your spiritual worship. Do not be conformed to this world, but be transformed by the renewal of your mind, that you may prove what is the will of God, what is good and acceptable and perfect." Rom. 12:1-2.

The *vita Christiana*, the Christian life, is by its nature a life lived through faith. It is the living out of freedom. Our methodological progression through the structural elements of the answer of living one's own life leads us to a consideration of the ethical nature of that life in its specifically Christian features. The question of what really can be considered to be specifically Christian can be answered from at least three points of view. It can and must be answered in the meaning in which Christianity is a historically distinct way of life derived from a specific historical starting point, that is, the life of Jesus and its consequences. Seen in relation to the fundamental debate of modern theology, this first observation verges on the banal. But at this point in our discussion it has quite basic significance for ethics. Whatever pretentions to universal validity can be reclaimed for Christianity can be reclaimed only as the consequence of a history of the effects that Christianity has had through the concrete way Christians have lived. Only that which has previously been a part of the way Christians have lived can claim validity here. The historical character of Christianity is in respect to ethics the historical scope of the Christian life. In as far as Christianity is, ethically speaking, a historical religion, the *vita Christiana* is the canon within the canon of Christian history. To state the issue in its simplest terms—without Christians there is no Christianity.

The question of what is "specifically Christian" can and must be answered in terms of whether Christianity has a well-defined ethics "all of a piece." Is there something that could be called a "civil code of the Christian community," a well-defined code of behavior with a normative body of rules for living, enforceable through sanctions and processes of decision making? The answer is no. But this no has a productive function, in that it offers a corrective to the question and modifies it by giving spiritual and theological meaning to ethical reflection. In reference to the New Testament, the *vita Christiana*, the Christian way of life, takes on in its own independent way the function that was formerly performed by the law. The freedom of the Christian life is based on a new and more intensive closeness in our relation to God. This is its specific Christian meaning, that is, the meaning demonstrated and made possible through Jesus Christ.

We may take this as a basic, unified feature of New Testament ethics. The sayings of Jesus in the Sermon on the Mount sharpen and intensify the meaning of the Jewish law for those to whom the law is addressed, active human beings with their views and opinions. But this leads to a renewal of the ethical meaning of the way we live, and it is no longer possible to confine this meaning to a body of laws. Paul's ethical teachings for community life, in which the words of Jesus play no direct, identifiable role, are Christian ethics for the living of life in the spirit of freedom. The attempt of the Roman Catholic Church, by means of an ecclesiastical law analogous to the old Roman law, to develop and impose a new law for the way Christians should live in general and in specific detail, has therefore no truly ecumenical validity for the whole of Christendom.

In addition to the works cited above on pp. 19–20, see also G. Bornkamm, *Die Bergpredigt Jesu*, 1962; L. Goppelt, *Theologie des Neuen Testaments*, 2 vols., 1974, 1976; U. Wilckens, *Rechtfertigung als Freiheit*, 1974.

The question of what is specifically Christian can ultimately become the question of the universality of Christian ethics and thus the question of its timeless validity. It is the question of the independence of Christian ethics from the passage of time and from the influence of the world in which we live. Whenever we set out to speak in a specifically Christian sense of the universality and independence of ethics, we then can and must bring what we say into relationship to the so-called eschatological orientation of the Christian faith. The issue is the ethical relevance of the hope and expectation of a future that transcends this-worldly time. Such hope truly involves a universal sense of freedom, because it does not accept the present world as the ultimate standard for the question humans ask about their true nature, but expresses in the symbol of the kingdom of God that this world, seen in light of a new creation, is destined to perish. To be sure, this eschatological faith is not a new formula for explaining the world. It is perceived and finds its validation through the leading of the Christian life, and therefore is only one element in the living of that life. Christians cannot and should not understand themselves as the agents of a new program for the world, a program that is to be brought into effect in this world. The freedom of the Christian life means, rather, that a Christian life is possible everywhere and at every time, and by its nature and its history contains the power through which an individual can change a world of apparently fixed conditions. The practice of the Christian life should express itself as the presence of the future in the present.

In the light of these presuppositions, it is now our task to show how the concept and the formation of the Christian life contains and integrates the various elements as set forth in the answer of leading one's own life.

Our first point of orientation is in terms of Paul's ethical themes. The occasion for personal ethical themes in the communities of Hellenistic Judaism is found in the practical issues of life. The hallmark of its historical genesis is not didactic, systematic deduction, but a line of argument through which the awareness of Christian freedom finds expression in an orientation for the way Christians lead their lives. This occasion can be characterized as a transition, an ethical crisis, a crisis of authority, which arose as a consequence of the insight that Christ is the end of the law.

This is the central content of the Pauline proclamation in Rom. 3:28, for example. Here the ethically relevant relationship with other persons, especially with one's fellow Christians, is no longer predetermined by the law, no longer established and defined. It must be given a productive form by means of the spirit of freedom. The crisis is also seen in the possibility of the abuse of freedom (1 Pet. 2:16; Rom. 14:1; 1 Corinthians 8, etc.). Paul had to define his position in debate with proponents of an understanding of freedom which sought fulfillment in acting without consideration for others. Faith, however, does not settle the question of how to live. This question constantly confronts us anew. Our conduct, the transformation of our lives, is to be accomplished as we lead the Christian life in the way that is proper to it. The way we live our lives takes shape in the debate with those who hold that living through faith places the Christian above ethics in this world. Here we can take note of Paul's argument, which assigns its proper place to the activity of leading a Christian life. In terms of content this involves the determination of the good, and testing and evaluating it in the spirit of those who are no longer concerned with establishing their own righteousness (Rom. 12:2; 9–21; Phil. 4:8).

The structure of ethical themes is determined by the task of making individually responsible decisions on the basis of principles. The misunderstanding of freedom arises when freedom is understood as self-determination. The Christian life is to be defined as a function of the reality of freedom. In other words, freedom of the individual Christian is not exercised in an absolute manner, but in the service of the community.

Thus the formula for the formation of ethics is called *oikodomē*, the "building up" of the common life. This gives added significance to the categories of moderation, of appropriateness, of faith in the common life, and of support and assistance to others. In this way the impulses and motifs of faith take the form of functions or offices in the community. The point of view of the formation of a plan for one's life become relevant for the Christian life, and through it the specificity of the life of faith comes to include the lively and concrete dimension of how we live with others and in community.

In this context we can consider the metaphor of the congregation as the "body" of Christ, which expresses not only the concept of the *unity* of the body, but in the paranetic passages also expresses the imperative for integrating one's own conduct into the "body" (1 Cor. 6:15; 10:16; Eph. 1:23, etc.). On the exegesis of the metaphor see the article by E. Schweizer in ThWNT VII (1964): 1024ff., as well as the supplement vol. X, pp. 1276ff.; also E. Schweizer, "Leib Christi and soziale Verantwortung bei Paulus," ZEE 14 (1970): 129ff.

Even though the origin of specifically Christian ethics is found first in the context of concerns within the community, the questions of relations with the outside world also play a significant role. In the questions of meat offered to idols (Romans 14; 1 Corinthians 8), marriage with unbelievers (1 Cor. 7:12), and going to the courts (1 Corinthians 6) we find conflicts which in the interests of leading a Christian life demand a more precise clarification of the relationship of the *vita Christiana* to the "world." Christian theology has been concerned with the dispute over whether the inclusion of the "world" in the understanding of Christian ethics arose as a proper concern of the church, or whether it was an unavoidable compromise that was unfortunately forced on the church because the expected end of the world did not take place, and the eschaton did not arrive.

It was E. Troeltsch especially who placed in the midpoint of his interpretation of this history of Christian ethics the view that Christian ethics in the age of the early church was a compromise (*Die Soziallehren der christlichen Kirchen und Gruppen, Ges. Schriften*, vol. 1, 1910, reprinted 1965; see esp.

pp. 83ff, 175–76 [*Social Teaching of the Christian Churches*, 1931]). But in his interpretation of this "compromise," Troeltsch let himself be too greatly influenced by the concept of an originally pure autonomy of the Christian faith in respect to ethics. This was an indirect consequence of his adopting in theory the modern understanding of autonomy.

In Paul's writings, ethical thought and reflection are where an awareness of the Christian conduct of life develops. Christians are to enter into a process of rational perception of what is good (Phil. 4:8; 1 Thess. 5:15; Rom. 12:9–21, etc.). In this connection, the view that one's personal faith is one's self-awareness of freedom is only an opinion. Rom. 14:22 says, in a characteristically pointed manner in the context of an ethical discussion, "The faith that you have, keep between yourself and God." In matters of ethics Paul pleads for a "freedom of opinion" that is preserved only where faith is not involved directly as an ethical argument, but is subordinated to the superior claims of the good. Thus his line of argument always tends to come out decisively on the side of the good (Rom. 13:13; 14:13, 10–12). An ethic of freedom is one in which Christians know themselves to be free in relation to their own faith, and can therefore be oriented toward human brotherhood.

The "inner" social nature of faith also permits it to have free access to the "outer social nature of our life in the world." The affirmation of responsibility for the world, as it came to be generally accepted in the church of the fourth and fifth centuries, had its specific presuppositions in the structure of ethics in the New Testament period.

A detailed historical exploration of this question is not possible here, because it can be dealt with adequately only in a history of ethics. See G. Kretschmar, "Welterfahrung und Weltverantwortung in der alten Kirche," *Die Verantwortung der Kirche in der Gessellschaft*, edited by J. Baur et al., 1973, pp. 111ff.

The acceptance of assigned roles and social expectations was not something alien and alienating for the Christian community because imposed from the outside. Rather it is the context in which life in this world as life in God's world makes it possible to discover anew the meaning of freedom as freedom experienced in life. Even the temptations that are involved are temptations that can be understood in terms of Christian responsibility for the world. In its organized ecclesiastical form Christian freedom can be greedy for authority, self-assertion, and worldly power, and can take on the stylized form of the moral superiority of those for whom all problems have already been solved and who therefore can assert an absolute claim to authority over the "world." As the corrective for this misunderstanding of the freedom that comes from Christian autonomy, the origin of Christian ethics provides ready arguments. Christian ethics is an ethics of yielding and of seeking to win others, an ethics of life in community and of responsible freedom. It is not an ethics of aggressive lordship over the world or of attempts to alter the world. Therefore it must struggle against those impulses within itself that push toward establishing a reign of law based on faith over the world. The microethical discussions of the Pauline community are thus repeated on the macroethical plane of the world church.

In all decisions involving ethical principles, in the formation of a life plan as a contribution to the formation of a common life, in taking over social roles, the Christian life implicitly expresses again and again the distinction between the living of one's own life and the activity of God. The Christian faith does not elevate the human moral agent to the position of God. On the contrary, it defines human beings anew in their personal and social, historical and political individuality in their relationship to God. This distinction implies an unconditional yes to the Christian's personal life, a yes that finds each one ready for that service to which we are called by the freedom that comes from faith. Thus it is a constitutive element of Christian ethics that the distinction between God and humankind plays a continuing role. Here we find the basis on which Martin Luther was led to combine the freedom which comes through justification by faith and the two ways in which God's rule is exercised. The doctrine of the two ways that God rules has as its basis in systemic theology the distinction between that which Christians are as a result of the gift of faith, and that to which Christians are called, as a result of that gift, to render through their own lives in service to God's world and in cooperation with all other human beings.

Following this reconstruction of the basic elements in the answer of leading one's own life, as they are integrated into the Christian life, it is necessary to pose the question, from what points of view can an ethic involve reflection on itself and knowledge of itself? What basis does it offer for a concept of the good, in relation to which the various elements in the structure of the ethic can establish their reliability and orderliness? This is the content of the next section, which is concerned with the various attempts to provide a justification for ethics.

c. The Task of the Theoretical
Justification of Ethics

What are the most significant points of view that play a role in the formation of ethics if we explore the task of a theoretical justification of ethics?

How does ethics arrive at self-knowledge? What are the theoretical bases that ethics takes into account in developing reflective thinking about itself? The objection might be raised that these questions have already been explored, and to some extent that objection would be justified. In exploring the components of the answer of the ethical tradition and the answer of responsibility ethics, it has become clear that we have encountered totally different approaches to ethical theory. The study of ethics can be hindered by the irritation produced by the multiplicity of theories that demand a hearing. This multiplicity has been allowed to express itself in such a way that the various distinctive aspects which are significant for the structure of ethics can be clearly seen. The multiplicity of theoretical efforts in ethics is not "merely" theoretical. It involves the complexity of the full range of ethical problems. Only against the background of this knowledge can we understand why the question of a theoretical justification of ethics is immanent in ethics itself and is not something that has been created for its own sake out of the need to pursue some argument.

A history or a systematic presentation of ethics that was concerned only to explore theoretical approaches could easily turn into a much larger review of the literature. And an ethics that was not aware of the theoretical aspects of the divergent themes involved, because it only dealt with certain interesting "cases" and investigated only the realm of concrete ethical decisions, is in danger of falling into an unconscious naivete.

We will now deal independently with the question of theoretical justification of ethics on the basis of the reason identified above (pp. 92–94), and will do so in such a way that ethical theory itself can be understood as a dimension of the ethical reality of life. This must be set forth in detail.

If the question is posed, why there are various theoretical approaches in ethics that result in contradictions and collisions, the answer is that various approaches to the formation of ethical theory represent distinctly different concepts of goals for the solution of the ethical task. An ethical theory always implies a specific concept of goals, in the light of which a specific solution of the ethical task can be formulated, and which is anticipated in the approach of that particular theory.

Is there a common point of reference for dealing with the various theoretical approaches? How can we avoid the impression that the matter involves a rivalry or a struggle for power among mutually exclusive theoretical observations? Various theoretical approaches in ethics resemble each other in that they always involve a specific concept of the goals to be achieved, goals in which it must be possible to discern something that they have in common among the diversity. The concepts of goals contained in the various approaches to ethical theory come into focus when the question is asked, What is the goal toward which the theory is moving? Every ethic is guided by a picture of a successful life, in which one's actual empirical life corresponds to the fullness of its possibilities, and in which the ethic is thus fulfilled. That which we have just formulated is a redefinition and new approach to the question of the "highest good," that is, the question of how the good is expressed in the form of that which is to be achieved.

The theme of a "doctrine of the good," or of the "highest good" was a distinctive feature of Schleiermacher's ethics. He presented it as a postulate in two addresses delivered to the Berlin Academy. In the writings published after his death it is clear that this postulate had great importance for the structure of his ethics (F. D. Schleiermacher, "Über den Begriff des höchsten Gutes," first presentation 17 May 1927, second presentation 24 June 1830, *Friedrich Schleiermachers sämtliche Werke*, third division, *Zur Philosophie*, 2 vols., 1838, pp. 446ff., 469ff. Also *Entwürfe zu einem System der Sittenlehre*, ed. O. Braun, 2d vol of the selected works, ed. O. Braun and J. Bauer, new printing of the second edition of 1927 in 1967. On Schleiermacher's ethics see especially H.-J. Birkner, *Schleiermachers christliche Sittenlehre im Zusammenhang seines philosophisch-theologischen Systems*, 1964; M. E. Miller, *Der Übergang. Schleiermachers Theologie des Reiches Gottes im Zusammenhang seines Gesamtdenkens*, 1970). Schleiermacher developed his demand for a structure of ethics which would be fulfilled as the "construction of the highest good" (first presentation p. 455) in a polemic against the "highly unnatural separation of activity and ways of acting from the works that result therefrom" (p. 451) and saw in this separation an absurd truncating of ethics. "If I don't want to accomplish anything, why am I acting?" Similarly he termed the idea of the highest good as that in which "production and product . . . are regarded as identical" (in his posthumously published lecture of 1812–13, *Ausgewählte Werke*, Band 2, p. 256).

Ernst Troeltsch, in a critique of the ethics of Wilhelm Herrmann, revived the demand for a doctrine of the highest good, and saw in it the union of ethics and philosophy of religion (*Grundprobleme der Ethik. Erötert aus Anlass von Herrmanns Ethik* [1902], in *Zur religiösen Lage, Religionsphilosophie und Ethik. Gesammelte Schriften*, vol. 2 [1913], reprinting of the 1922 second ed. in 1962, pp. 552ff.; W. Herrmann, *Ethik*, 1901. On Troeltsch, see W. Pannenberg, "The Basis of Ethics in the Thought of Ernst Troeltsch," *Ethics*, Eng. trans. 1981, pp. 87–111).

The new discussion of the question of the "highest good" has in this present context the purpose of redefining the concept, as we use it methodologically to achieve clarity about the goals advocated in the various theoretical approaches in ethical discussions. We are using it as a methodological tool for entering into the debate required in ethics with various approaches. In this way, the theoretical debate can be concentrated in and limited to a point of view that is relevant for ethics itself, without the necessity of exploring the extensive basic debates involving approaches in the social sciences, philosophy, and theology found in every question concerning basic theory.

If we assume, as has been said above, that the various approaches in ethics result from differing concepts of goals, then it may be hoped that by working back from these concepts we may learn something about the relevance which these approaches have for ethics. To be sure, this is not possible without selecting a few examples from among the approaches under discussion today. This will enable us to limit the points of view of the methodological path on which we have set out. The following five points can be derived from the five elements which were discussed in the development of the first two possible answers.

1) The Satisfaction of Needs: The Revival of Hedonism in Critical Theory

Every ethic has its vision of the successful life, which portrays the correspondence of the actual, empirical life and the wealth of its possibilities. In connection with this vision it is inevitable that the limitations which hinder this correspondence should be discussed. The perception of the goal is thus present in the criticism of a world that interfered with their accomplishment. In so far as ethics or specific historical forms of morality itself are included among these limitations, morality is called "repressive." If the achieving of the goal requires active human participation which must take place outside those limitations, there is talk of a "new" morality or ethics. The theoretical justification of ethics, in both criticism and affirmation, draws its arguments from the goal of a successful life, because the goal is anticipated only through theory, and only so is it brought into accord with the reality of experience.

A vision of the successful life which has enjoyed tremendous popularity in recent years is contained in the program of a satisfying of needs, with the critical overtone of "universal" gratification of "true" needs. In the complex political and social debates of recent times, in which the slogan "revolution" has been invoked repeatedly, we find a moral claim that appeals to the satisfaction of needs for its justification. The ethical situation of the present day includes a lively revival of hedonism. "Pleasure," "happiness," "desire," and their satisfaction are the key words in this renaissance of a doctrine of happiness which claims human nature as the theoretical justification for deciding what can be considered ethics and what must be subjected to criticism. The distinctive theoretical profile of the so-called critical theory, as advocated by Herbert Marcuse, is that it has been committed to a revival of hedonism. Here is found in all the clarity anyone could desire the model of a "highest good" that has demonstrated its attractiveness in a great variety of modifications and applications in the minds of both young and old.

As early as 1938, in his paper "Zur Kritik des Hedonismus," Herbert Marcuse developed the basic outlines of that which later in the student movements from 1966 on gave to his statements a force specifically suited to the times (H. Marcuse, "Zur Kritik des Hedonismus," *Zeitschrift für Sozialforschung* VI, 3, Paris 1937, reprinted in H. Marcuse, *Kultur und Gesellschaft* I, 1965, pp. 128–68, and now in H. Marcuse, *Schriften* 3, 1979). A concise definition of "critical theory" is to be found there: "Under the term critical theory, we understand the theory of society, as it was presented in the principal essays in the *Zeitschrift für Sozialforschung* on the basis of dialectical philosophy and the criticism of political economy" (note 18, p. 178). See also the essays of M. Horkheimer in the same journal, which A. Schmidt collected and edited. (M. Horkheimer, *Kritische Theorie*, 2 vols., 1968).

Marcuse interprets the hedonistic tendencies in ancient philosophy as a protest movement which arose in opposition to the conflict seen between happiness and reason. The major ancient philosophers as well as the philosophers of German idealism rejected the claim to happiness as incompatible with reason. But Marcuse is not motivated by an interest in the history of philosophy. "By the principle of hedonism the demand for individual freedom . . . was brought into the realm of the material conditions of life.

In so far as an otherwise proscribed facet of human liberation has been preserved in the material process of hedonism, it is the result of interest in critical theory" (p. 130f.). This renewal of hedonism brings a new definition of the goal. Happiness is to be found through satisfying desire, which, as something material, bodily, sensuous, is also the criterion for general rational knowledge which corresponds to human nature in general. Ancient hedonism, to summarize Marcuse's argument, concentrated on the fulfillment of direct, individual needs and desires. In opposition to the limits imposed by conventional morality, he asserts that we should satisfy our desire or desires as often as possible. The only thing is enjoyment; that is the only happiness that is appropriate for an individual. Marcuse regards this hedonism as "progressive" (p. 134), because it does not conceal its opposition to general rationality, but instead proclaims it. But ancient hedonism had no social consciousness of the necessary conditions for attaining this result. Marcuse prefers this "unmediated" or "positive" hedonism to Epicureanism, which permits only a specific, measured sort of desire. It is a "negative hedonism," because its principle is more to avoid the unpleasant than to achieve pleasure, an "avoidance of the conflict with the existing order" (p. 138). Marcuse's goal is to strengthen the sensuous against the authority of reason, and as a result he criticizes the belittling of the sensuous by philosophy as an expression of a repressive society, where "the satisfaction of drives and needs" is in "bad repute" (p. 149). In any case, modern society, oriented as it is toward production, has opened the door to a world that provides room for the demand "that each individual should share in the products of society according to his needs." "Through the many-sided development of individuals and of the power of productivity, society can now inscribe on its banner, 'from each according to his abilities, to each according to his needs.' Here we find again the ancient hedonistic definition that happiness consists in the manifold satisfying of needs" (p. 151).

Ancient hedonism had a plausibility that was always capable of renewal, because there was a constant and immediate nexus of experience between needs and their pleasurable satisfaction. It was this immediacy of direct sensual experience that gave to the pleasure principle its special status, which was not subject to a general principle of truth. The happiness of the moment of pleasure is complete in itself. Marcuse now wants to capture hedonism for his general understanding of truth. He can do this only by stressing the distinction between "true" and "false" needs. In this manner critical theory separates the concept of happiness from its dependence on the direct individual experience of pleasure. For under present social conditions individuals can have only "false needs."

The higher insight of critical theory makes it possible "to regard factual, actually experienced happiness in previously existing conditions as untrue" (p. 159). Critical theory takes the place of human beings as the "judge" of their happiness, since they are "hindered from the knowledge of their own real interests" (p. 160). This is the claim that critical theory asserts. "Hedonism is abolished in critical theory and practice" (p. 167). The struggle for this higher universality of the future in the present "becomes the cause of special individuals and groups." For the paradoxical human situation "is apparent to only a few" (pp. 165–66).

The renaissance of hedonism through the development of critical theory by Marcuse can no longer be justified in a hedonistic manner. Human happiness needs an advocate who fights for this happiness, even, if necessary, against the (corrupted) will of human beings. The reconciliation of needs with their satisfaction through the experience of pleasure can be brought about only by means of the theory, that is, by the advocates of the true satisfaction of needs, who are guided by the knowledge of the truth and thus are representatives of "the self-determination of liberated humanity in their common struggle with nature."

Marcuse carried his program of a renaissance of hedonism as the responsibility of critical theory further in his discussion of Sigmund Freud (H. Marcuse, *Eros and Civilization*, 1955). His critique of Freud's reality principle follows the same pattern as the critique of the subordination of the pleasure principle to philosophical reason. He posed the question of whether sexual drives, given free rein, constitute an equivalent of the limits of the satisfaction of pleasure in Freudian theory, and then speaks of a "libidinous morality" which as an ethic after the sexual revolution formulates something that could be called "sensuous rationality," "and made eros accessible in the freedom of order" (p. 227). But this would be conceivable only in an "order of plenty," of superfluity (p. 193). "The social condition for happiness is an eschatological totality of liberation" (H. Ringeling in his debate with H. Marcuse, "Christliche Ethik im Dialog mit der Anthropologie: Das Problem der Identität," in *Handbuch der christlichen Ethik*, vol. 1, 1978, pp. 482ff. esp. 487). In this way "ethics is finally abolished" (ibid. p. 487).

From this renaissance of hedonism in critical theory it is now possible to draw an important conclusion for the possibility of a theoretical justification of ethics out of the concept of a "highest good." The concept of a "highest good" makes ethics inoperative, if this concept is taken as a direct guide for conduct, that is, is placed on the same level as the actual living of life. The logical conclusion is then that the attainment of the highest good makes ethics superfluous and unnecessary. This raises an old theological problem, which has always been dealt with in the relation of human and Christian ethics to the concept of an eschatological kingdom of God. Those who regard themselves as functionaries of the "kingdom of God" make themselves the standard of that kingdom in the "kingdom" of their own real activities. In place of the real freedom of those humans now living we find the theory of their liberation from this world of theirs. But ethics only apparently loses its function. For the difference between the "now" of the problematic empirical reality of life and the "sometime" of the fulfilled life must always be kept in mind. And it is kept in mind by those advocates of the "highest good" who recommend themselves to others as those who can lead them into true life. The problem of ethics becomes a problem of the elite who want to lead others into a new realm of life. In this situation the question of the justification of ethics is reduced to the question of the justification of those who in the struggle for the realization of the highest good stand on the right side and in this struggle appear as the "good" against those who are "evil."

Marcuse saw this clearly. For him ethics was the explicit theme as an "ethics of revolution" (Marcuse, "Ethik und Revolution," in *Kultur und Gesellschaft* 2, 1965, pp. 130–46. Compare the discussion in my article, "Ethik und Revolution," in T. Rendtorff and H.-E. Tödt, *Theologie der Revolution*, 1968, pp. 99–113). Marcuse subsumes the question under the ethical hypothesis that "good" is that which serves to produce, promote, and extend human freedom and happiness in a common life (p. 130). The problem is stated: "Can the use of revolutionary force be justified as a means for establishing or furthering human freedom and happiness?" (p. 132) If ethical standards are valid as historical standards, then the "ethical and moral right" which is claimed by a revolutionary movement is to be measured by whether its "means are appropriate for achieving this purpose." The question of the ethics of revolution "appeals to a historical calculation": Can "the society which the revolution envisions offer a better chance for progress in freedom than the existing society?" This requires an accounting of the resources and of the means to use these resources. A sketch of this sort can offer no objective criteria for determining whether revolutions are progress or regress "in reference to the development of humanity" (p. 141). But this calculation is simply a comparison of the sacrifices demanded. Marcuse speaks quite objectively of these sacrifices. The "sacrifices" which result from the existing society should be compared with the "sacrifices" which the revolution demands in order to achieve its goals. Who are the ones offering the sacrifices and who are the ones being sacrificed are questions that remain unanswered. For the sacrifices are a factor in the calculation. The legitimation of the revolution depends entirely on its "purpose," the liberation, or the maximizing of happiness. But, "the purpose must be at work in the repressive measure necessary to achieving it" (p. 146).

By this line of argument it becomes clear that Marcuse makes ethics into a function of a collision of goals. The question of what relationship exists between the "existing" society and a "new" one that is to be ushered in by revolution is viewed by him as only the relationship between "given conditions" and "other conditions," but he does not relate them to the human beings who live in these societies and who constitute the conditions. His thesis is: "Moral measures, on the basis of their imperative claims, transcend every given circumstance" (p. 141). The permanent obligation, if it were to be applied to the ethics of revolution, cannot be identified with the revolution. The revolutionary claims must themselves be subjected to the critique of obligation and therefore cannot lay claim to a position that cannot be transcended, in relation to which the future and the existing situations must equally play a role in the historical calculation. The decision as to which "situation" of human nature is the more adequate implies, on the contrary, for Marcuse a moral decision that cannot be determined by the goal, that is, the "highest good," but it turns the ethical decision back to the subjects who are to lay claim to this goal for themselves. In relation to the "highest good" the individuals who are involved do not find themselves in the same situation. Those with "insight," by virtue of their concept of the goal, can exercise moral authority over those who "lack insight." They do not, however, do so by virtue of the lives they are leading, but in the name of the universal nature of their goal. In this way the "highest good" becomes a partisan issue and ceases to be a universal point of reference for ethics.

The problems and difficulties inherent in the theoretical justification of ethics attempted here in terms of the goal of a free satisfying of needs is involved with the very fact of the content assigned to the goal itself. If the "highest good" is to be identical with that which humans claim for themselves as the "highest good," it loses any meaning it has as a point of orientation, and becomes merely a function of a theoretical and practical egoism of self-realization, however sublime. Of course the goal would be attained if all needs were met. That would indeed be an ultimate situation for which ethics would be superfluous. The abrogation of ancient hedonism, which limited itself to the satisfaction of desire through the desires, resulted in the goal becoming a partisan instrument for the mode of life of those who used it against others for their own benefit. In the struggle over a life appropriate to the "highest good," this "highest good" of necessity loses its meaning as a critical point of orientation. And in this way it becomes subject to the alternation of success and failure in the process of liberation.

Schleiermacher, who formulated for us the question of the "highest good," had already progressed beyond this point (*Die Christliche Sitte*, ed L. Jonas, 1884, General Introduction, pp. 36ff., esp. 39–40). He defines desire as the impulse for "community with God." "In absolute blessedness (as community with God) there is no impulse (to act), because we cannot conceive of it except in terms of all activity having here been completed." The difference between need and satisfaction is abolished. But this difference is precisely the place where ethics comes into play. The relationship between "desire" and "no desire" plays a role in the "developing" blessedness, in the relationship between approach to blessedness (desire), and the negation of blessedness (no desire). We experience as "desire" everything that brings us closer to blessedness, and as "no desire" everything that separates us from it. Both no desire and desire are the theme of the difference from blessedness, not as an absolute difference, but only as a relative one, because it is related to blessedness and is determined by it alone.

Only when we comprehend that the principle of desire in all its forms, even in the form of longing for fulfillment and liberation, expresses the theme of this difference, does it become clear that ethics addresses itself to human beings, bidding them to orient themselves and their world toward the achievement of "happiness." But ethics is not the means for realizing the "highest good" as such. It describes the way by which humans shape and should shape themselves and their world in relation to "happiness." But if the highest good is the completion of all activity and thereby the abolition of this difference then it cannot itself be taken into account in our activities as one "situation" in opposition to other "situations." This anthropologizing of the highest good will of necessity destroy the humane meaning of ethics. If there is to be a justification of ethics by means of a theory of its goal, this goal must have a content that is determined in such a way that it is and remains distinguishable from autonomous human activity. The goal of "satisfying needs," even if these are "true" needs of human beings, is not such that it can still maintain this distinction.

2) *Truth as Truthfulness: On Analytical Ethics*

"The meaning of the world must lie outside it. In the world every-thing is as it is and occurs as it occurs. There is no value in it, and if there were it would have no value." "Therefore there can be no ethi-cal statements. Statements cannot express something higher. It is clear that ethics cannot express itself." (Ludwig Wittgenstein, *Tracta-tus logico-philosophicus* [1921], 6.41; 6.42.) These apodictic assertions of Wittgenstein's do not, of course, mark the end of ethics as scientific theory, but they do very clearly mark a difference in its perception, as it divides the analytical philosophy practiced in England from con-tinental philosophy.

"What is occurring in English and Scandinavian philosophy has nothing at all in common with the concerns that occupy German and French philoso-phy. Each of these two philosophical directions lives in its own world as if the other did not exist" (K.-E. Løgstrup, "Ethik und Ontologie," ZThK 57 [1960]: 377. See also his "Betrachtungen über die englische Moralphilosophie des 20. Jahrhunderts," ThR, NF. 39 [1975]: 139–55).

It is not merely a sense of duty to chronicle these movements that leads us in this discussion of various approaches to the theoretical justification of ethics to examine analytical philosophy and the ethi-cal theory derived from it. What we can learn in the process will serve to help us define more precisely a goal of ethics that is quite dif-ferent from but not without connection with the question which we are pursuing in this investigation of the doctrine of the highest good. In order to understand the significance which metaethics has for ethics we must consider the critique which it brings against philosophical idealism. (In addition to the writings of Bertrand Rus-sell, the most significant work is G. E. Moore's *Principia ethica*, 1903). [*Principia Ethica*, 1959].

This critique seeks to make clear that between a philosophical system of thought and that which we can determine to be real, including every-day human knowledge, there is a deep chasm. Ethics cannot be developed in isolation from the reality of language as it is actually spoken. Instead, ethics must be subjected to the control of experience that is generally accessible.

Logical positivism rather quickly and consistently concluded that ethics was linguistic nonsense. Analytical moral philosophy, on the contrary, made a broad and intense attempt to provide a theoretical justification for ethics. Through an analysis of language the attempt was made to find the basis of ethics in ethics itself, that is, in the use of moral words and concepts. However this may have turned out in detail — and we will look at that shortly — it is clear that we have here a quite different approach to the question. The goal is not a "completion" of the ethical task beyond the reality of actions and their linguistic expression. Almost nothing is said of this in analytical ethics. This becomes quite clear in the approach by examples drawn from minute realms of activity in the world of daily life, the here and now of human activity. The merchant on the corner, the automobile salesman, the money lender are examples that are fully adequate to illustrate the "goal" of analytical ethics.

Any comprehensive critique of "conditions" in the world is completely foreign. The manner of speaking and the examples chosen make clear that the theoretical goal is a certain and clear knowledge of our own ethical judgments, such that when the will that sets norms and makes decisions is subtracted from the equation, these judgments can be determined to be reliable and justifiable by the form in which they are stated. This is an application of the goal of a theoretical justification of ethics to the expression of ethical speech, truth as truthfulness. This is also the reason why, since the time of Moore, writers have spoken of a metaethics that is to be distinguished from normative ethics. We can term this method a "goal" because it attempts to achieve an accuracy and certainty of ethical argumentation which is based on itself and is therefore not dependent on other goals of specific nature and content. In a certain sense this reinforces the concept that "ethics" is *always* encountered and is therefore encountered in quite differing situations in history and in every-day life. The issue then arises as to whether there is an independent form, a structure of ethical speech, that can be construed as an independent element of the human conduct of life.

In this century it was G. E. Moore who initiated the discussion of the meaning of moral terminology, in his *Principia ethica*, 1903. A significant further development of his ethical theory is found in his book, *Ethics*, 2d ed., 1966. It appeared in German translation in 1975 as *Grundprobleme der Ethik*, with a fine introductory foreword by Norbert Hoerster, pp. 7–17.

Moore's explicit concern was to establish the independence of ethics from empirical and metaphysical explanations. He contended that moral philosophy had totally failed to achieve a correct analysis of the ethical question, and insisted that it is necessary to draw a fundamental distinction between two questions that had previously been confused. The first is, what type of actions should we undertake? And the second, what things should we do for their own sake? The answer to the first should tell us what type of actions will lead to there being more good in the world than would result from any possible alternative action. The second, which is to be distinguished from it, would clarify what things should exist because they are in themselves (intrinsically) "good." In drawing this distinction Moore is concerned that a utilitarian concept of ethics confuses these two aspects when it says that that which promotes something good is therefore good in a general and self-evident sense. But according to Moore this is a naturalistic fallacy. For example, when I say that "good" is what produces development or a recognizably useful result, then "good" is defined by statements that relate to facts. Such theories he calls definition theories, because they seek to define the understanding of "good" or "correct" as an empirical fact.

In opposing the definition theory, Moore objects that it rests on a "naturalistic fallacy." This is demonstrated by the objection of the so-called "open question." If "good" is that which promotes development, then what promotes development? And further, why is what promotes development "good"? The conclusion is false because the real ethical question is not only not answered, but remains unasked. This objection should make it clear that the definition theory assumes that which is to be proven. The certainty of the ethical judgment, its justification, is simply assumed and not logically arrived at.

In contrast to definition theories, Moore holds that the judgment as to what is "good" is self-evident and cannot be derived from an empirical definition of a condition. Therefore he argues for the judgment "good," and therefore for ethics in general, that there is a distinct epistemological status, by which we "intuitively" know what is "good." An ethical judgment with the word "good" is possible only if it has meaning in itself, and can therefore be used as a criterion for such questions as, what is likely to produce development? This position of Moore's, which is shared by a number of other philosophers, is called intuitionism. The fundamental principles of morality are self-evident for ethical insight, and can therefore quite obviously be taken as our basis for forming ethical judgments.

The further discussion of this assumption produced two lines of argument which have given more precise structure to ethical decision making and have provided a correction for Moore's position, without thereby invalidating his goal.

Good introductions to the quite diverse literature on this subject are A. MacIntyre, *A Short History of Ethics*, 2d ed., 1968, pp. 249ff.; A. Montefiore, *A Modern Introduction to Moral Philosophy*, 3d ed., 1968. Useful works in German are H. Fahrenbach, "Sprachanalyse und Ethik," in H.-G. Gadamer, ed., *Das Problem der Sprache*, 1966, pp. 369–85; A. Pieper, "Analytische Ethik. Ein Überblick über die seit 1900 in England und Amerika erschienene Ethikliteratur," *Philosophisches Jahrbuch* 78 (1971): 144ff.; A. Pieper, *Sprachanalytische Ethik und praktische Freiheit*, 1973.

The first objection points out that the assumption of an intuitive ethical insight leaves unexplained why this insight should move us to act in accordance with it. The other objection points out that even in a case in which something is intuitively recognized as obviously good, there must be criteria that would enable us to distinguish such a judgment from another, in contrast to which it is good, or of which it can be said that it is not good. In what respect is something obviously good? These two objections have led to new attempts to construct metaethical theories quite different in nature, and which in the course of the discussion have led to new incentives in the formation of a "practical philosophy."

The first objection was raised by C. L. Stevenson in his *Ethics and Language* (1944) in the following way. The evidence of the intuitive judgment "good" is not a judgment about a "good" that is self-evident. It is merely the manner in which I express the direct feeling that something appears good to me. But then the function of the statement that something is "good" is that I would like to convince others to regard it in the same way. What can be discerned in the verdict "good" is not an intrinsic meaning of "good," but the intention to move others to adopt the same opinion. These are judgments that express an emotive position. Thus we can speak of emotivism as a consciously non-cognitive theory. The judgment "X is good," means then, "I am in favor of X, and you should be too." The expression of value is a descriptive component, in which the speaker communicates his own position in reference to X. And it also has an imperative component, by which the one addressed is to be brought to the same position. The result is then that ethical statements have the function of influencing others in respect to actions and persons. The accurate description of actions or persons is a means of influencing or convincing others. Thus the negative statement, "You shouldn't lie," is also a linguistic expression of the emotive position, "Phooey on lying!"

This results in a situation in which it is not possible to argue about imperatives, but only about the description of that which is to be regarded as "good" or "bad." Moral discourse then consists in trying to convince others of the validity of one's own description of reality. The difficulty this poses for emotivism is that moral discourse is reduced to convincing others to accept one's own position. This explanation is directed only to the secondary use of moral judgments. It is not the primary use of the words "good" and "bad" that has meaning, but only their use to convince others. To this extent Stevenson also makes an important assumption. He assumes that one's own value judgment is based on a spontaneous or emotional position that is not subject to further questioning. But definitions of ethics as attempts to convince others are no justification for an ethical judgment itself. For before a "You should" can be spoken, an "I should" must first be formed, from which an "I want, and others should too" can follow. The communication of the ethical decision for one's own ethical position is not one of Stevenson's themes. But in reference to Moore, Stevenson has called it to our attention that descriptive expressions are always morally evaluative expressions as well, or that moral language also involves a descriptive meaning.

Here we encounter the second objection that has been raised against Moore's intuitionism. It says that what Moore intuitively assumes as "evident" in a given case actually appears as evident only in a specific historical context, and is therefore dependent on a historical relationship. This argument is directed toward the blindness of metaethics to history. The "evidence" is limited to a present situation of understanding, to a relatively closed group of data. And it cannot bear the weight of an argument for a generally valid epistemological status of ethics that goes beyond the individual. This argument can be expanded to an ethical relativism that is in principle only in relationship to a specific historical situation, which is experienced together with a specific and limited number of other persons. Then the question of a basis for the theory has departed from the realm of ethics. It becomes a matter for a science of history or a philosophy of history. In this case the metaethical goal of an independent ethic is not eliminated, but the necessity arises of searching for another, higher, or more complex metatheory. The objection can be so constructed that it becomes an argument for ethical pluralism. But the question of what claim to universal validity one's own decision possesses can no longer be answered. On the contrary, from the position of ethical pluralism the conclusion can be drawn that this question no longer need be answered, even that it is a false question, because ethical judgments are always dependent on their being carried out in life, and it is only there that they have independent status.

This objection was principally formulated by A. J. Ayer, *Language, Truth and Logic*, 17th ed., 1967, and R. G. Collingwood, *The Idea of History*, 1970.

This objection notes that in reality it is always the case that varying ethical evidence is taken into account, and one bit of evidence is in conflict with another. Thus the only way to maintain an independent and sure judgment is to say it ultimately involves a decision in favor of a specific model for living. This decision is a condition for being able to live in an ethically responsible manner in a situation of ethical pluralism.

A. Jeffner's position in "Die Rechtfertigung ethischer Urteile," ZEE 19 (1975): 234–48, ends in just such a pluralism. H. G. Hubbeling introduced the expression "communicative mode" in order to show that the connection between "is" and "should" appears in the very act of speaking ("Einige Probleme der analytischen Ethik," ZEE 15 (1971): 20ff.).

In his later writings Wittgenstein ascribed great significance to the mediating of descriptive and prescriptive language of morality by the central concept of "language game." He interpreted human actions in terms of persons talking with one another. Life is carried out in speech, speaking is a "form of living" (Wittgenstein, *Philosophical Investigations*, 1953, p. 24). The term "language game" emphasizes that speaking a language is part of an activity, or of a form of life. Acting and speaking are the two elements that constitute life. The theory of "language games" says that language has a variety of functions, but they are known to us only when we take part in the game. Each language game can be comprehended in its context only by those who play it and follow its rules. There are "resemblances" among the various language games, which Wittgenstein characterized as "family resemblances" (p. 48). We see a complicated net of resemblances that cross and overlap one another. There are greater and lesser resemblances. The differing resemblances are to be thought of as being like those among members of a family: height, facial features, color of eyes, gait, temperament, and so forth. And thus the "games" constitute a "family." The common point of reference of all language games is then, however, conversational language as the ultimate language of life, behind which we cannot go.

Hare's definition of the relationship between principles and decisions has been discussed above (pp. 123–26). His line of argument is quite similar to that of Wittgenstein's language games, insofar as principles have their authority in a specific context formed by one's upbringing. Hare goes further at a decisive point when he says, "When I acknowledge a principle, I am not determining a fact but rendering a moral decision," that is, I make myself "in an important sense responsible for the judgment" (*The Language of Morals*, 1952, p. 196).

Thus in a certain sense the line of argument, though altered, returns to its starting point. For even intuitionism finally means that though a moral judgment cannot be deduced, it is not merely a subjective view that we happen to prefer, but it derives its evidence from its content, which places us under obligations which demand recognition. These obligations cannot be demonstrated purely as such, independent of specific life situations or historical contexts, but only by being lived out in those situations and contexts.

The goal of metaethics is to find a solution to the ethical task in which the "good" validates itself. This solution, however, is not sought in a life beyond, but in the conduct of our own individual life. The discussion above has revealed the extreme theoretical difficulties and dilemmas that this involves. In formulating the dominant concept of the goal, no one has been able to eliminate the historical conditions and contingencies of the contexts in which the "good" asserts itself in the living out of an individual life. And that is not the intention. The weakness of analytical ethics is at this point its strength. For it asserts something that must always be said about the situation of ethics, that its independence can only be shown when truth is perceived and recognized in the form of individual truthfulness. It is not those who want to do good in general, but those who want to do good themselves, who can know what it is that ethics is talking about.

This specification of goals makes it possible to distinguish between a "highest good" and "good" in one's own life by bringing into play for one's own ethical standpoint only one's own moral and intellectual responsibility. The defining of limits includes not only the necessary openness for the processes of forming ethical judgments together with others, but also the openness to comprehending what one recognizes as "good" in relationship to a "good" about which nothing can be said in the sense of a "highest good," since it is not at the disposal of those who live with one another and speak with one another, and therefore cannot be used as a weapon in the struggle with others in order to win for oneself a moral superiority that, in any case, is only apparent.

Thus the justification of ethics is related in a specific respect to a "theological" type of argument which P. Lorenzen termed the "*inaccessability* of reasonable and peaceful life together" (P. Lorenzen and O. Schwemmer, *Konstruktive Logik, Ethik und Wissenschaftstheorie*, 1975, p. 13). A life in the light of a "highest good" would not then be one that attempted to claim the "highest good" absolutely and to achieve it, but one that is lived in relationship to others and to one's self in an ethical manner in recognition of the good and in the expectation that this would also be done by others.

3) The Ideal Community of Communication: Practical Philosophy

"The anticipation of the ideal situation for speaking together has for all possible communication the significance of a vital gleam of light that is the harbinger of a way of life" (J. Habermas, "Vorbereitende Bemerkungen zu einer Theorie der kommunikativen Kompetenz," in J. Habermas and N. Luhmann, *Theorie der Gesellschaft oder Sozialtechnologie*, 1971, p. 141).

In the concept of the goal of "non-authoritarian communication" we can recognize a key element in many expectations of morality or of social criticism which are at work in the emotional background of discussions specific to the present epoch concerning existing and "new" society, and which are articulated in various, even self-contradictory theories of action that are always intended to be practical. It is not surprising that in this the concept of an unforced community of communication plays a prominent role. Even apart from all the interests involved, it is in the logic of a theory of ethics to think of its justification in terms of the concept of freedom, so that the concept of a universally good situation involves participation in that good situation, and that means participation in bringing it to pass. Thus communication is an obvious key word, because it implies action as the relationship of persons to one another in a situation where they talk with one another, and which can be conceived of as a "free," unforced communication in which the "good" is the common good, freely striven for. To this extent communication as the ideal community of communication is a key that is searching for its keyhole.

It is not necessary to traverse the whole range of theses and proposals which are involved in this key concept. We will limit the discussion to the approach to ethics which is justified by this criterion of a "highest good" in the community of communication, and to the insights that can be gained in this way for the structure of ethics. More precisely stated, we will limit ourselves to the arguments of recent practical philosophy in the narrow sense.

Thus we will not take into account the large number of articles and discussions collected by Manfred Riedel in *Rehabilitierung der Praktischen Philosophie*, vol. 1, 1972; vol. 2, 1974, but will look instead at the arguments developed by K. O. Apel as well as by P. Lorenzen and O. Schwemmer. (K. O. Apel, "Das Apriori der Kommunikationsgemeinschaft und die Grundlagen der Ethik," in *Transformation der Philosophie*, vol. 2, 1973, pp. 358–435, published in condensed form in Oelmüller, Dölle, and Piepmeier, *Philosophische Arbeitsbücher, 2d Diskurs: Sittliche Lebensformen*, 1978, pp. 321, 343; P. Lorenzen, *Normative Logic and Ethics*, 1969; P. Lorenzen and O. Schwemmer, *Konstruktive Logik, Ethik und Wissenschaftstheorie*, 1975).

The concept of a "non-authoritarian discourse" developed by Habermas resulted from the concern which political ethics took in the question of how to draw anew upon the tradition of politics as promoting the "good life" in opposition to the forces of technological and scientific rationalism. He insisted that "two concepts of rationalism must be kept separate": The rationalism of scientific and technological progress that provides "rational, goal-oriented actions" and the rationalism found in the "medium of interaction through speech." But in historical and practical terms this requires a "removal of limits on communication" in the sense of an "unlimited, non-authoritarian discussion" (Habermas, *Technik und Wissenschaft als Ideologie*, 1968, pp. 48–103, esp. p. 98). The assumption contained in such a demand must then be that we attain insight, through communication, into the "good," and that communication through language can be the place where the "good" is present.

Following the line of argument developed by K. Popper, the founder of critical rationalism, P. Lorenzen developed the objective, systematic connection between logic and ethics. This idea was taken up by K. O. Apel. The significant thesis here is that "logic . . . presupposes an ethic as a necessary condition for its existence" (Apel, 329).

The rationality of logic is the rationality of practical logic, which gives to language its status as a means for achieving interpersonal understanding. Anyone who uses language as a means of communication is involved, because of the logic inherent in language, in interpersonal communication, and affirms that this is so because otherwise it would not be possible to use language at all. But this logic which is immanent in language and through which it is used is not neutral. Indeed there is an "ethics of logic." This "ethics" is that of a community of communication which belongs to the language itself, and is not something added by the will of those who speak it. The logic of language, the condition for its being understood, is as logic structured so that understanding takes place, and that means that it is ethically structured. Thus far Apel is speaking of an ethical "apriori of a community of communication" in reference to logic. In this general sense it can be accepted that "speaking" is in specific cases participation in the general good, by virtue of the ethics immanent in the logic of language.

Since this involves the logical structure of language and that alone, for those humans who are actually using language it involves the setting of a goal, that of an ideal community of communication. This brings to the fore a difference that cannot become thematic without revealing a specific tendency. The presupposition immanent in the ethics of logic is nothing other than that which is found in the logic of language itself, that is, it is independent of the views and position of those speaking, those who take part in communicating through language. It consists solely of the interpersonal, objective nature of the logic of language. Thus we can say, "In the community of communication the mutual recognition of all members as equally valid partners in the discussion is presupposed" (Apel, p. 330). This formulation reveals the problem of how the "ideal" community of communication is related to the "real" community of communication. If this "ethics of logic" is applied to the central question in our investigation into the determination of goals in the sense of a "highest good" and its function for providing critical orientation, then the ethics inherent in the logic of language must represent the goal of successful communication, that is, communication in which ethics finds fulfillment in the successful, logical use of language.

Both Apel and Lorenzen and Schwemmer have developed from this an ethics for the application of the ethics of logic, an attempt that confronts us once again with the question of what significance it has

for ethics when we take as our goal the "highest good." Apel formulated the "demand for mutual recognition of persons as the subjects
of logical argumentation," and extended this to demand that it
include the recognition of "all" persons, because "all beings who are
capable of communicating through language" can be "in all their
actions and utterances potential partners in the discussion," and the
"unlimited justification of thinking cannot exclude any discussion
partner and that partner's potential contribution to the discussion"
(p. 330). From this universal demand Apel develops the "tran-
scendental-pragmatic conditions" (p. 331) of a basis or justification of
ethics, which justifies the opinions of everyone by the claim which
"each member of the communication community has on all the
others." This, he insists, is a "moral duty," which involves not only the
duty to "employ logic" (p. 332), but goes much further in imposing
"the duty of taking into account all the potential claims of all potential members," and that means then "all their 'needs', in as far as they
might make claims on their fellow human beings" (p. 335). From this
Apel develops the "long-range moral strategy by which each human
being should act," the effort "to make real in the actual world the
ideal community of communication" (p. 340). We must therefore sacrifice our egoistic subjectivity to this moral strategy in the interests
of the "trans-personal" (p. 336).

If we reflect on these demands, it is clear that the theoretical
justification of ethics tends toward the direct realization of the goal
that has been set. It imposes for the realization of the empirical,
"real," community of communication demands which cannot be fulfilled by the means at the disposal of the empirical individuals who
are involved. Who could be able seriously to take into account "all
others" and their claims, or even claim that we should want to do so?
Instead of a reasonable delimitation of ethics in terms of a "highest
good" in the form of an ideal community of communication, Apel
demands that we attain to unlimited communication. The postulate
of a "realization of the ideal community of communication" is, as a
program for removing all limits, tied to the commandment that we
should in principle attain to "moral self-transcendence."

This direct combining of the ideal community of communication
with the reality of linguistic communication by the demand that it
be completely realized discredits the theoretical assumption of an
ethics of logic. The ideal community of communication is made
dependent on its being realized, and thereby it loses its function of

providing critical orientation. In this context when Apel uses the concept of an "emancipation strategy," it can only be the emancipation from real communication in the interests of the ideal. This realization of the ideal is then the negation of the only human reality that is ethically relevant. The eschatological concept of boundless communication, if it is made into an oral demand, abolishes its ethical meaning. The real task would be to show that the concept of an "ideal" community enables us to achieve a conscientious, ethical, and logical grasp of specific, limited communication and specifically how it is possible for us to do so.

The problem which confronts us here anew is that of the content of communication. Apel has nothing to say about this in his purely formal argumentation. A limitless communication which followed all the conditions that Apel stipulated could only be communication about content, which also encompassed and set forth thematically the conditions over which living, empirical human beings and the real community of communication have no control, and which therefore they do not confront as direct demands to be fulfilled. That is the specific content of religious communication, which in its symbolic formulations sets the theme of the difference between that which humans are commanded to do through their acts or through communication in the specific contexts of life on the one hand, and on the other limitless communication with "everyone" as ultimately successful communication, seeing that as the difference between a life that is caught up into the life of God and a life in the world in the presence of God.

In the light of this distinction between the content of the "highest good" in the concept of "ideal communication" and that in actual human communication, it is possible to develop a meaningful ethics of communication. But in order to do so, the content of the communication must play a role if we are to grasp the difference between "ideal" and "actual" communication in its function for ethics. Then it can be said that human communication, by virtue of language which is not under our control, but which is the only means through which we can speak, already partakes of the "ideal." Precisely for this reason, the knowledge that we participate in communication through language obliges us to follow the "ethics of language" in limited communication which is related to specific persons and to content that demands responsibility, and which is valid in its very concreteness. At the same time, we are freed from the obligation always to be trying to accomplish something totally different — ideal communication. The difference of context which is crucial here becomes clear only when we are aware that the same language can be used to speak of different things — different in the sense of that which is appropriate for human activity, and that which is not at human disposal but must still be taken into account. The well-intentioned ethical demand on the community of communication that it realize the "ideal" community might well, instead of making possible specific and responsible communication, unleash the terror of the demand for total communication and thus turn the critically oriented truth of the "ethics of logic" into its opposite.

The task which Lorenzen and Schwemmer assign to ethics is expressly limited to the "actual" community of communication, that is, "establishing principles for overcoming conflict," as far as this can "be accomplished through speech in a manner that can be taught" (p. 150). The goal of ethics is identified as the "overcoming of conflicts." Philosophical interest in ethics is limited to the development of didactic terminology for dealing with conflicts that arise when "mutual opposition hinders the achievement of the goals being pursued" (p. 149). Where there are no conflicts there is no need for ethics, that is, argumentation has no practical purpose.

When we survey the suggestions that have been made in this approach to ethics in individual cases with the intention of developing a detailed discussion, the first impression is that there is no need for any additional definition of goals, and ethics can be reduced to developing reasonable rules for discussion in order to resolve conflicts of purposes as they develop in situations of disagreement. But even this approach involves defining goals of ideal communication that require interpretation through the assigning of tasks in a pragmatic manner. The decisive means of overcoming conflict is the process of consultation (pp. 159ff.). Even Lorenzen and Schwemmer say that those involved in conflicts are by no means necessarily those who are in a position to represent their cause effectively and clearly and to take part in the process of consultation. The terminology of philosophical ethics is valid only for those "who are competent to take part in meaningful consultation." But the competence which is required here is not merely the linguistic competence of one trained in philosophy. It also involves knowledge of the conflicts that are to be discussed. This entire dimension is relegated to the "theory of practical knowledge," which as "interpretation of culture," "criticism of culture," and "reform of culture" develops elements for a reconstruction of the social world, and ultimately has as its theme the knowledge which is the necessary condition for competent consultation. But in this way all the problems find their way back to ethics, which was supposed to be rendered unnecessary here by being limited to the rules for argumentation. If we wish to hold on to a limited theory of ethics, there must be a normative definition of goals that includes more than the idea of overcoming conflicts. Limiting the discussion to this goal gives the impression that it would be good to limit our consideration to those conflicts that can be resolved. These then would have to be distinguished form conflicts which involve those contingent differences among persons in their relationships to each other that are characterized by personal freedom, and which if they appear to be resolvable are not to be dealt with through the "liquidation of those ways in which we differ from one another" by simply removing those differences from the world. The area of ethics must be defined in such a way that its goals include the concept of freedom, which is relevant for the evaluation of conflicts if it includes not only the overcoming of conflicts but also the limitation on efforts to overcome conflicts while recognizing their existence. The extension of the goal of overcoming conflicts to include recognition of conflicts cries out for the presence of the "ideal" community of communication in the real community, not with the goal of a total homogenization of situations of conflict, but by recognizing their relative status. This goal implies a concept of a "highest good" which is modified to become a theory of social institutions that relativizes conflicts, and that places limits on unresolvable conflicts in a manner which promotes freedom.

On the basis of similar considerations, H. Lübbe called pragmatism the "art of limiting discourse" ("Pragmatismus oder die Kunst der Diskursbegrenzung," in Oelmüller, et al., op. cit, pp. 344ff.). This points the way to an approach to ethics that finds expression in a sociological theory of morality. (See volume 2 of this present work.)

If we think the consultation model through to its logical conclusion, the question in its dominant statement of goals becomes focused on the competent observer, that is, the one who has such a comprehensive and non-partisan overview of the entire situation as to be able to survey and evaluate the conflicts between various goals and interests in the light of what is common to them all. This means that we must think of consultation as a situation in which those involved are able and ready to lay their own interests aside for the duration of the consultation, and who are also able to command the practical knowledge involved in its totality.

In his characterization of the "original position," John Rawls developed an ethical consultation model and sought to make it operational. In this process he drew on the concept of an "ideal observer," as developed by R. Firth (J. Rawls, *Theory of Justice*, 1971). Firth established the following criteria for the ideal observer:

1. He is omniscient in respect to the totality of factors relevant to the situation. The ideal observer knows the total situation; he is, so to speak, the all-knowing expert.

2. He is omnipercipient. His imagination or ability to perceive is comprehensive. He can anticipate what effects specific decisions will have and can so project himself into the future context of the results of decisions that they can be taken into account in making the decision.

3. He is disinterested. Just decisions must essentially be non-partisan. The ideal observer represents the total interest of the whole.

4. He is dispassionate. The struggles and the emotional factors arising in the context of conflicts, which become irrelevant only when a just decision is reached, play no significant role for the ideal observer in the search for the ideal decision.

5. He is consistent. The ideal observer has the ability, in the framework of arriving at a just verdict, of achieving resolution, not case by case but continuously (R. Firth, "Ethical Absolutism and the Ideal Observer," *Philosophy and Phenomenological Research* 12, 1952, pp. 336–41).

These criteria describe the character of a just judgment in the cases that give occasion for ethical consultation. The place of such a hypothetical construction of an ideal observer is clear: It involves an ethico-theological construction. Naturally the practical consequence is not that people should act as if they were God, but that they should make use of the knowledge that they are not. Obviously the situation of those involved in ethical consultation is not that of the ideal observer. Moreover a rational model for consultation without such a "theological" implication would not be rational. In applying an ethic of communication it is essential to distance oneself from the situation of conflict which is to be resolved, and this should be done by making oneself accessible to those seeking counsel. This is possible only if it is kept in mind that their situation includes more than those issues that are to be considered. It is in this direction that the critically oriented appeal of a "highest good" in theological terms can serve ethical communication.

4) Freedom Beyond Society: The Basis of Morality in Systems Theory

Is there ethics only for those who are willing to be subject to the rules of consensus? Is non-conformity only the exceptional borderline case in ethics? Anyone who says yes can also say no. In contrast to the communication model as a basis for ethics, the question must be raised whether ethically relevant participation in communication does not have a parallel theme in which a person distances him or herself from communication. The basis of ethics in communication theory carries with it the latent tendency to draw a distinction between those who act with good will and those who act with bad will, and to assert the moral right to secure the boundary of its explanatory power. What is involved here is the meaning of the concept of freedom for the basis of ethics. Wherever the question arises in the theoretical argumentation of communication doctrine as to whether it is permissible to force everyone to participate in a rational community of discussion, we become aware of a problem whose weightiness first forces itself fully on our attention when we look at it in analytical and metaethical terms and do not bedeck it with the moral verdict that it should not be a problem.

How can freedom as a goal of ethics be brought into play in such a manner that it takes on meaning for the critical orientation of ethics both as a concept and as a concrete issue? Clearly not so that freedom designates the material task whose accomplishment is the content of ethics, that is, as a command to produce freedom and to equate it with specific relationships among persons. Freedom as the goal of ethics must be so thought of that freedom remains free and thereby becomes relevant for ethics as a basic feature of its structure.

The systems theory which N. Luhmann developed under the influence of Talcott Parsons led, through its consistent use of the functions of sociality, to freedom as the precondition for morality, a precondition that does not become absorbed as one of the empirical constituents of the moral life, but comprises the "environment" of each specific morality.

Luhmann thus made constructive use of his central thesis of system functions for moral theory. He asserted that the social system works without

individuals as persons, because it is adequately defined through its social
functions and relationships, for which the individual person is not a constituent, but merely represents an external relationship. (On Luhmann's thought
and especially this thesis, see, "Religiöse Dogmatik und gesellschaftliche Evolution," in K.-W. Dahm, N. Luhmann, and D. Stoodt, *Religion, System,
Sozialization*, 1972, esp. pp. 37–38; "Sinn als Grundbegriff der Soziologie,"
in J. Habermas and N. Luhmann, *Theorie der Gesellschaft oder Sozialtechnologie*, 1971, esp. pp. 25–100. On the debate with Luhmann from the side
of theology, see E. Herms, "Sinn als Grundbegriff der Soziologie," in ZEE 13
(1974): 341–95; F. Wagner, "Systemtheorie und Subjektivität. Ein Beitrag zur
interdisziplinären theologischen Forschung," in *Internationales Jahrbuch
Für Wissens- und Religionssoziologie* 10 (1976): 151–79; T. Rendtorff, *Gesellschaft ohne Religion*, 1975, esp. pp. 36ff., 75ff.). On the problems of the basis
of ethics in terms of systems theory, see especially, N. Luhmann, "Soziologie
der Moral," in *Theorietechnik und Moral*, 1978, pp. 8–116. This is the source
of the quotations that follow. Luhmann used here exclusively the term
"morality," because he wanted to produce, through the sociology of moral
relationships and institutions of society, a new discussion of that which I have
here included under the term "ethics."

Luhmann subjects the "anthropocentrism" of the "old European"
moral theory to a critique insofar as this theory "has dealt with
sociality as a property of humanity," and thereby was led into
"socializing and historicizing humanity, including even its theoretical
value" (p. 37). If humanity, in the sense of the Aristotelian *zoon
politikon*, is "by nature a social being," then the consequence for
modern critical social theory is that under the pressure of the increasing anonymity of social relationships it can only cite the humanity of
humankind in opposition to the existing state of society. If sociality
is conceived only in anthropological terms, then "humanity" must be
presented as an alternative program in contrast to the existing society,
because the "moral reality of society" (Habermas) is understood as
the necessary realization of human morality, and humans find their
own purpose fulfilled in sociality. Luhmann denies that this is an
adequate theoretical concept of morality, just as his sociological systems theory is a thorough critique of the anthropologizing of the concept of society. He also denies the direct coupling of social morality
with the realization of the moral person. The weight of this critique
becomes clear when we consider the effects it has for a metaethical
theory of morality.

In terms of systems theory the following conclusions can be drawn.
"Social systems arise whenever persons enter into relationships with

one another." Morality exists in the relationships and in the form they take, and nowhere else. "Individual persons constitute the environment of their relationships to each other and also in relationship to the social system that develops. They do not merge with one another or with the social system" (p. 43). Individuals are not absorbed into society. Their independence functions as the contingent "environment" for social relationships and the systems which they form. If, on the contrary, we were to proceed from the theoretical premise that human sociality is identical with one's own "natural purpose," then such a distinction would be inconceivable. It would also be inconceivable how it could be demanded that humans take a position toward the morality of social relationships, unless it were only in such form that the structure of social relationships not yet or no longer corresponded to the true social nature of human beings. In terms of the theoretical premise alone there would then result a situation in consequence of which the moral claim on society would always have to be that of a moral critique. This is a highly important objection, because it points out that in such theoretical premises the theory itself obliges us to engage in moralizing.

It is possible to speak of the independence of morality in an analytical, metaethical sense that seeks a firm basis only if morality can be distinguished from the "person," if the person constitutes his or her own "system" in contrast to the social system. The distinction introduced here, however, does not require that a distinction be drawn between the moral person on the one hand and the actual social relationships on the other hand, but that it be drawn between moral social relationships and the person. Only social relationships are morally relevant; morality exists only as social relationships. But the person is never identical with specific social relationships and must therefore be distinguishable from them in theory. This is supported by the distinction between social system and "environment," and the person as environment of social systems. If we ask then in what way the person is involved in the morality of social relationships, and how that morality is determined by the fact that it is the relationship between persons, then the answer which Luhmann gives is contained in the expression "respect" (*Achtung*). Morality is a "manifestation of respect" (p. 52).

Respect, according to Luhmann, is an expression of mutual acceptance that is more elementary than consensus, because respect also includes lack of consensus. Respect defines mutual acknowledgement in the realm of social relationships, which constitute the subject matter of morality; it is not the moral quality of persons, but their relationships that form its content. In contrast to totalitarian moral demands, the category of respect has the advantage of defining morality in terms of the actual relationships in the social system in which it has its own place. In this it is not necessary that the entire complex background of the quality of persons be a part of the theme. This definition also expands the concept of morality, because the regulation of social relationships can also be included, relationships that are not exhausted in consensus, agreement, and self-realization. If morality is real in social relationships in which mutual respect finds expression, then it places obligations on the persons only in so far as they actually are involved in social relationships with one another. Respect is a morally immanent category which must not place obligations on the totality of the personality. "Respect can be developed in the same degree that freedom can be presupposed." "A morality that rests on respect is a consequence of freedom." A part of showing respect is therefore "tact" (p. 55) as the avoidance of direct and immediate confrontations involving persons, that is, tact as "metamorality." Respect as the basis of morality lets one consider the freedom of the persons involved and has freedom as its presupposition (p. 59). This at once allows us to explain that the morality of the social system can remain flexible, because in the relationships neither the being nor the non-being of persons is involved at all, so that moral change in the historical or sociological sense as change in specific social relationships can be pictured much less dramatically and need not be presented each time as a totally new moral situation, or as a summons to morality. To this extent metaethical theory makes it possible for moral theory to hold much closer to empirical reality.

If freedom is the pre-condition for respect, and respect the basis of morality, then freedom is the basis of that morality which in the sense of a theoretical setting of goals allows us to distinguish between the task which confronts ethics and the basis for it, which we must take into account. Ethics must therefore not be regarded as the realization and thus the abolition of its goal, but as being based on and critically defined through its theoretical concept of goals. Luhmann sees freedom specifically "as the result of socio-cultural evolution, with the intention of watching for and warding off the "moral interest in intensifications of freedom," as that interest gained entry into ethics on the track of idealistic concepts of freedom (p. 61). Whether it is necessary to cite the increase in complexity of social evolution is a question of the interpretation of socio-historical processes, which we do not intend to explore further here, nor is it necessary to do so.

For the basis of morality it is necessary to apply freedom as the base of respect to the person itself, and the person comes into consideration as the contingent "environment" of others and of specific social systems. Luhmann dealt with this "self-reference" as being the necessity of "self-respect" (p. 48). In carrying forward the argument in terms of systems theory, this leads to the individual persons allowing respect to be expressed toward themselves, that is, placing themselves in a relationship to themselves in which they are not only at one with themselves, but are able to distinguish between themselves as persons deserving of respect and their "environment," that is, the freedom in respect to which they are persons. This distinction, however, points precisely in the same direction as the goal of the theological basis of ethics. In reference to oneself, respect is demanded as "self-respect," because persons in their personhood have a basic freedom which is not exhausted in their self-realization and is therefore not fully realized in their actions. Freedom of the person, as was said earlier in this book, is in the theological sense always freedom which we have received from others. It has its primary reality in the relationship of human beings to God, which enables us to have "respect" for the person, and to have self-acceptance independent of deliberate attempts to succeed in life. Luhmann expressly did not follow out this line of thought.

In relation to others, however, "respect" can take on the meaning of consciously accepting in one's own actions responsibility for being the "environment" for others, and thus of doing more than is required in specific social relationships and according to their morality. In our terminology, this is a case of reflective ethical thought, which gathers together and expands "morality" and its basis. This reflection of respect leads to love, in the maxim "that the lover as the one who loves can be the environment which the beloved needs" (p. 70). Love is expressed then, not by the direct consensus between the lover and the beloved, their personal unity, but by the world which they need in order to live. In this way the systems-theory basis of morality comes to include freedom through love as part of its context in a manner equivalent to what happens in the theological basis of morality. It is then consistent and appropriate for Luhmann to insist that love itself cannot "be moralized or even honored moralistically," because it is precisely here that the always problematic "unity of love and morality" cannot be theoretically implied, but the distinction between the basis of love itself in freedom and the activity of love in the context of the moral environment of the person plays a role (p. 71).

In the area of systems theory it becomes clear once again that a distinction must be drawn between the foundation of ethics, as it can be set forth in its theoretical definition of goals, and the task of ethics in respect to the empirical conduct of life. It should be reiterated that this is why Luhmann, in reference to the latter, speaks only of morality in the sociological interest of investigating the sociology of morality, in the tradition of "moral science." Ethics as ethics must play a role in defining its basis and therefore must expose this distinction. The question which Luhmann consciously passed over is that of the basis of freedom itself, as that freedom must be presupposed for the basing of morality in the act of according respect. Working out a basis of freedom that is relevant for morality but is itself "independent of morality," is a prominent theme of a theological justification of ethics.

5) *The Coming of the Kingdom of God as the Theological Goal of Christian Ethics*

When we inquire into the theological justification of ethics, what goal plays the decisive role? What concept of the goal of Christianity in terms of its origin (both in terms of its historical origin and of its systematic starting point) is theology to stress? How does this goal function as a justification of ethics?

The various approaches of ethics which have been examined here in terms of their goals are to be included in our answers to these questions, both in terms of method and of content. Each in its own way takes a point of view, some on the basis of content (fulfillment of nature, ideal communication in justice) and others on the basis of function (language, freedom of the person in relation to the social system) as the standard for a critical orientation of the definition of the ethical task. As a provisional resume of the methodological structure of ethics it can be said that the goal of ethics functions also as its justification if it fulfills a double task. It makes ethics possible when it addresses persons in terms of the distinctive features of an existing situation in which they live and act. It presents a possible way of doing ethics when it places the ethical task in the perspective of a goal that provides an orientation for that task.

In contemporary theology the question of a theological justification of ethics has concentrated on the definition of goals expressed in the concept of "kingdom of God."

This has by no means always been the case, nor has the intensity with which it was presented been the same. Only in response to Johannes Weiss,

Die Predigt Jesu vom Reiche Gottes, 1892, did it become a generally accepted historical judgment in theology that New Testament eschatology was to be highly esteemed as the decisive basic orientation of the proclamation of Jesus and of the early church. The acceptance of this judgment in systematic theology, and especially in ethics, through a general use of the category of eschatology, especially the symbol of the kingdom of God, took place in a specific historical setting. See G. Sauter, *Zukunft und Verheissung. Das Problem der Zukunft in der gegenwärtigen theologischen und philosophischen Diskussion,* 1965, esp. pp. 84ff.

We will first ask which historical and systematical problems in the discussion of a basis for ethics in theology led to this renaissance of eschatology.

In modern theology a great deal of importance has attached to an approach that speaks of ethical obligation, which, in a certain sense is immanent in human, but also in moral, historical, and politico-social relationships. The basis of ethics then takes the form of a doctrine of the Law of God, which inheres in the world as God's creation and is therefore binding on humans. This leads to talk of ordinances and mandates which confront humans in the form of secular, social, and historical responsibilities and which are regarded as duties. The trans-personal nature of ethical duties is then seen as the theological basis of ethics. The question of humans as subjects of ethics is regarded as valid only in this setting and is not raised in any independent manner.

In modern theology there has been a significant opposing view, which explicitly distinguishes the Christian life from the given ethical responsibilities which are immanent in the world. The basis of this ethical position takes the form of a doctrine of the gospel of Jesus Christ, which frees men and women from the world and places on them only one duty — to fulfill the faith. The discussion then concerns the special will of God that is revealed in Christ, living as Christ's disciples, new obedience, and the role of the church as witness to the world. It is then Christology that defines ethical responsibilities.

These theological basic orientations relate in opposite ways to the relationship between "Law and Gospel," a basic form of Reformation theology. Contemporary Lutheran theology, especially that represented by the Erlangen theologians P. Althaus and W. Elert, but also by H. Thielicke, and to some degree by F. Gogarten, stresses in its systematic development of the basis of ethics the precedence of Law over Gospel. Karl Barth, on the contrary, reversed the terms as "Gospel and Law" and in so doing stressed the exclusive superiority of the revelation of Christ for all other knowledge of reality, especially the authority of grace over law. Many have followed him in this, especially E. Wolf and W. Kreck.

It is questionable whether this dispute has been waged at the right place and over the right questions. In any case, the position which gives precedence to the Law must answer the question of what positive role the "Gospel" plays in the defining of a basis for ethics. Similarly christological theology must answer the question of what value worldly experience of ethical reality has. The partially polemical charges, "Law without Gospel" and "Gospel without Law," point to theological dilemmas. The "Lutheran" position, contrary to its intention, was forced in the direction of a methodological and technical dualism, as the result of which a "worldly ethic" and a "Christian ethic" stand unrelated to each other. An especially clear case is W. Elert, *Das christliche Ethos*, 1949.

It is then difficult to explain what common and comprehensive theological orientation can deal with the distinction between Law and Gospel in such a way that they do not end up being separated. The christological approach is forced by its premises to subsume Law completely under Gospel, with the result that the Gospel itself takes on the appearance of Law. An unlimited perception of ethical phenomena cannot be rejected in favor of an ideology of Christian norms. This approach has difficulty explaining how there can be such a thing as an ethically relevant meaning of reality as creation.

The problems of the "Lutheran" position become especially clear in the development given it by H. Thielicke in his *Theologische Ethik* I, 3d ed., 1965. "Ethics is an emergency discipline after the fall" (p. 609). The historical situation of humanity before God is that of life in a fallen world. The ordinances governing life in this world are "emergency measures." They disclose their normative function by reacting against human folly. The world of sin is a world that needs ethics. Its ordinances as emergency measures partake of ambiguity in that on the one hand they were instituted by God against the fallenness of the world as the miracle of the preservation of the world from sin. On the other hand they are themselves expressions of the fallen world, and are necessary because of the sin of the world. The "Christian" nature of ethics can only indirectly be a theme, that is, an awareness that the world is fallen. But the presupposition on which such an awareness is based must logically and in terms of its content be a knowledge of the goodness of God and of the good. Thielicke made this presupposition into a feature of a world view, since the reality of the world in theological terms is determined solely by its fallen nature. The christological transmission of this world view has no status of its own for the foundation of ethics. Thus in reference to the conduct of life it does not come into play, because life is lived in the fallen world.

Bonhoeffer clearly identified the problem when he pointed out that the result of such an ethic is that it tries to deal with the concept of two differing realities (E. Bethge, ed., *Ethik*, 1949, pp. 55ff.). The dilemma was that of a world without Christ, and a christology without a world. Bonhoeffer set up the contrasting thesis, "There is only one reality." That is the reality of God in the reality of the world as revealed in Christ. For Bonhoeffer the theme of ethics is the "reality of Christ's becoming reality." Bonhoeffer tried to deal with this in a concrete manner by transforming the static concept of ordinances into the concept of "God's mandates," which are given to us as tasks to perform (70ff.).

If for Karl Barth "the knowledge of the unconditional sovereignty of the grace of God" (*Kirchliche Dogmatik* II, 2, 1942, p. 566) has unconditional priority, this logically leads to the elimination of the ethical task. "In that God makes himself responsible for humans, he also makes humans responsible. Sovereign grace is imposed grace. The Gospel itself and as such has the form of Law. God's one word is Gospel and Law. . . . It is Gospel according to its content, Law according to its form. It is first Gospel and then Law" (p. 567). As a consequence of this the content of the christological basis of ethics must remain completely open. It is concerned only with "enabling humans to act" with their "liberation" and thus turns the ethical verdict over, in a large degree, to religious preference. (For a critique of this view see M. Honecker, "Das Problem des theologischen Konstruktivismus," ZEE 24 [1980].)

Against the background of these conflicting definitions, the orientation to the eschatological symbol of the kingdom of God has attracted new interest as the theological basis of ethics. It provides a point of reference that includes both world and the ethical subject, that is, it provides orientation to a goal that can overcome the apparent theological conflict between the doctrine of creation and Christology.

The most recent renaissance of eschatology was represented in Protestant theology by J. Moltmann (*Theologie der Hoffnung*, 1964, 1976 [ET *The Theology of Hope*, 1976]). For Moltmann eschatology takes on directly normative significance, with the result that the eschatological orientation of faith seeks fulfillment as a sort of Christian counterpraxis against the existing world. Eschatology functions thus not as a basis for ethics, but as if it were itself a normative ethic.

Paul Lehmann developed an eschatological theology of history in a different manner as a frame of reference for ethics. It leads through a messianic Christology and ecclesiology to an "indicative" ethics, the indicative of which is to become relevant in participation in God's revolutionary, world-transforming activity (P. Lehmann, *Ethics in a Christian Context*, 1963). Lehmann provided the theologically important stimulus for the "theology of revolution," as presented first by R. Shaull, though without any interest in a theoretical foundation for his position ("Revolution in theologischer Perspektive," in T. Rendtorff and H.-E. Tödt, *Theologie der Revolution*, 1968).

Serious reservations must be voiced against these attempts to form a normative eschatological ethics, because the distinction between ethical criteria for human life and action and religious goals that transcend human action could not and can not be defined.

For a critique, see for example, J. Baur, "Geschichte und Eschatologie in socialethischem Aspekt," in *Die Verantwortung der Kirche in der Gesellschaft*, ed. J. Baur, L. Goppelt, and G. Kretschmar, 1973, pp. 31ff. Inasmuch as the basic theoretical presuppositions were not discussed in the controversy, it was carried on largely in a quite political manner. The appeal to the two-kingdom doctrine and its essential distinction between the two ways in which God rules therefore appeared to be predominantly political resistance to specific ethical demands of action programs formulated in eschatological terms.

Quite distinct from these approaches is the manner in which W. Pannenberg sought to introduce eschatology and the concept of the kingdom of God into the discussion of the basis of ethics. Pannenberg accords to eschatology a metaethical status and introduces it into ethics by a highly differentiated phenomenological understanding of eschatology. See especially his article, "The Revelation of God in Jesus of Nazareth" in *Theology as History*, ed. J. M. Robinson and J. B. Cobb, 1967, pp. 101–33, and his *Theology and the Kingdom of God*, ed. R. J. Neuhaus, 1969, especially the chapters "The Kingdom of God and the Foundation of Ethics," pp. 102–26, and "Appearance as the Arrival of the Future," pp. 127–43.

The contents of the arguments advanced in the rich and varied concepts of the proclamation of the kingdom of God can be summarized succinctly. Jesus' message speaks of the kingdom of God and its coming. "The coming Kingdom of God — this was the single pulsating reality of Jesus' existence" (W. Pannenberg, *Theology and the Kingdom of God*, 1969, p. 102. The sentence quoted here was omitted from the German translation, *Theologie und Reich Gottes*, 1971). The concept of the coming of the kingdom of God brings into play a future that is then reflected in the expectation of faith. This future accords only temporary status to each situation in the world and to any action directed toward the future. This temporary nature of the world is the basis for distinguishing between human beings and their world and characterizes them in relation to the world as independent, responsible subjects. This is the function which eschatology has of providing critical distance for ethics. The expectations of faith relate to the content of the kingdom of God, which lies in the promise of complete community with God and the fulfillment of every search for the good. This content forms the basis for the trustworthiness of the search for the good beyond any human success or failure and allows human expectations, which in all activities helps shape the theme of an ultimate goal of action, to participate in ultimate success. That is the function which eschatology has for ethics: providing orientation and encouragement.

To be sure, eschatology can be misused as the goal of ethics. The concept of a coming kingdom of God can fall into a sharp dualism of "this" (perishing) world and the coming world, and in this way produce a strong defense against disappointments through the suffering of the world, a defense which can only mean resignation. Ethical interest on the other hand can become the subject of the coming kingdom and end up in the slogans of a radical and unlimited demand for change that negates "this" world. In both cases eschatology does not serve as a theological justification and basis for ethics, but takes direct possession of the role of ethics.

Eschatology cannot itself be ethics and cannot take the place of ethics. It makes ethics possible and demands that it be practiced. As doctrine of the "highest good" it represents the completion of the ethical task, but it does so in a theological manner. An eschatology that is understood as an alternative ethics loses its significance for critical orientation. It will inevitably lose itself in the vastness of unlimited demands which it is unable to restrain and which need to be corrected by ethics.

If the extensive and complex historical and systematic concepts of eschatology are to function in defining goals, then they must be reduced to elementary form in the context of the ethical argumentation. The meaning of eschatology for the justification of ethics can be seen when it is interpreted in terms of the two basic elements of ethics which have been used here as the starting point for the investigation of ethics: The givenness of life and the giving of life. In reference to these two basic elements of the ethical reality of life, eschatology sets the theme of an ontological "added value." The givenness of life includes more than can be comprehended through human experience and active acquaintance with reality. In its significance for creation it points to a perfected creation, renewed in relationship to the world of human concerns. The giving of life contains more than can ever be expressed in specific purposes and goals of human activity. In its meaning for life it points to a perfected, renewed community that goes beyond any specific definitions of goals. But active human beings can not simply identify themselves as the subjects of this ontological "added value" of the givenness of life and the giving of life. The true subject is recognized when God is acknowledged as the subject of all reality. Taking the coming of God's kingdom as our goal brings the ontological "added value" of reality into clear view in a theological manner, this is, in its orientation toward God.

In this theological definition, eschatology makes ethics possible by confining it within the boundaries of an independent human task and freeing it from the burden of wanting to be something other than the study of how human life should be lived.

The relationship of the ethical task to the future and the possibility of accomplishing it does not, however, become immediately relevant, that is, relevant by the exclusion or negation of actual human life or of responsibility for life. The symbol "kingdom of God" has its significance as an enduring encouragement to do the good that transcends success. It is a goal, the attainment of which embraces human actions and human achievement of the good, because it can appeal to the desire to accomplish the highest good. Its success is always anticipated in a liberating manner in one's own success, and is thus the basis of our human freedom to act.

Eschatology as the definition of our goal has its hermeneutical locus in Christianity. The history of Christianity is the context in which the eschatological hope is handed on. In opposition to a superstitious, concrete expression of the eschatological expectation, we must today emphatically establish that Christian eschatology can portray the ethical meaning of Christianity by transcending historicity in the history of Christianity, but in keeping with its intention is perceived again in the context of that history. In this sense the theological basis of ethics points forward to the concrete applications of ethics.

Index of Subjects

Index of Authors

191